# ICE CREAMS, WATER ICES, FROZEN PUDDINGS

# ICE CREAMS, WATER ICES, FROZEN PUDDINGS

**Together with**

# Refreshments for all Social Affairs

**BY MRS. S. T. RORER**

**Author of Mrs. Rorer's New Cook Book, Philadelphia Cook Book, Canning and Preserving, and other Valuable Works on Cookery**

KALPAZ

ISBN: 978-93-5128-941-8(HB)

First Published in 1913
Indian Reprint in 2017

*Published by*

Kalpaz Publications
C-30, Satyawati Nagar,
Delhi – 110052
E-mail: kalpaz@hotmail.com
Website: kalpazpublications.com
Ph.: +91-9212142040

# Contents

# Foreword

## CONTAINING GENERAL DIRECTIONS FOR ALL RECIPES

In this book, Philadelphia Ice Creams, comprising the first group, are very palatable, but expensive. In many parts of the country it is quite difficult to get good cream. For that reason, I have given a group of creams, using part milk and part cream, but it must be remembered that it takes smart "juggling" to make ice cream from milk. By far better use condensed milk, with enough water or milk to rinse out the cans.

Ordinary fruit creams may be made with condensed milk at a cost of about fifteen cents a quart, which, of course, is cheaper than ordinary milk and cream.

In places where neither cream nor condensed milk can be purchased, a fair ice cream is made by adding two tablespoonfuls of olive oil to each quart of milk.

The cream for Philadelphia Ice Cream should be rather rich, but not double cream.

If pure raw cream is stirred rapidly, it swells and becomes frothy, like the beaten whites of eggs, and is "whipped cream." To prevent this in making Philadelphia Ice Cream, one-half the cream is scalded, and when it is *very* cold, the remaining half of raw cream is added. This gives the smooth, light and rich consistency which makes these creams so different from others.

## USE OF FRUITS

Use fresh fruits in the summer and the best canned unsweetened fruits in the winter. If sweetened fruits must be used, cut down the given quantity of sugar. Where acid fruits are used, they should be added to the cream after it is partly frozen.

## TIME FOR FREEZING

The time for freezing varies according to the quality of cream or milk or water; water ices require a longer time than ice creams. It is not well to freeze the mixtures too rapidly; they are apt to be coarse, not smooth, and if they are churned before the mixture is icy cold they will be greasy or "buttery."

The average time for freezing two quarts of cream should be ten minutes; it takes but a minute or two longer for larger quantities.

## DIRECTIONS FOR FREEZING

Pound the ice in a large bag with a mallet, or use an ordinary ice shaver. The finer the ice, the less time it takes to freeze the cream. A four quart freezer will require ten pounds of ice, and a quart and a pint of coarse rock salt. You may pack the freezer with a layer of ice three inches thick, then a layer of salt one inch thick, or mix the ice and salt in the tub and shovel it around the freezer. Before beginning to pack the freezer, turn the crank to see that all the machinery is in working order. Then open the can and turn in the mixture that is to be frozen. Turn the crank slowly and steadily until the mixture begins to freeze, then more rapidly until it is completely frozen. If the freezer is properly packed, it will take fifteen minutes to freeze the mixture. Philadelphia Ice Creams are not good if frozen too quickly.

## TO REPACK

After the cream is frozen, wipe off the lid of the can and remove the crank; take off the lid, being very careful not to allow any salt to fall into the can. Remove the dasher and scrape it off. Take a large knife or steel spatula, scrape the cream from the sides of the can, work and pack it down until it is perfectly smooth. Put the lid back on the can, and put a cork in the hole from which the dasher was taken. Draw off the water, repack, and cover the whole with a piece of brown paper; throw over a heavy bag or a bit of burlap, and stand aside for one or two hours to ripen.

## TO MOLD ICE CREAMS, ICES OR PUDDINGS

If you wish to pack ice cream and serve it in forms or shapes, it must be molded after the freezing. The handiest of all of these molds is either the brick or the melon mold.

After the cream is frozen rather stiff, prepare a tub or bucket of coarsely chopped ice, with one-half less salt than you use for freezing. To each ten pounds of ice allow one quart of rock salt. Sprinkle a little rock salt in the bottom of your bucket or tub, then put over a layer of cracked ice, another layer of salt and cracked ice, and on this stand your mold, which is not filled, but is covered with a lid, and pack it all around, leaving the top, of course, to pack later on. Take your freezer near this tub. Remove the lid from the mold, and pack in the cream, smoothing it down until you have filled it to overflowing. Smooth the top with a spatula or limber knife, put over a sheet of waxed paper and adjust the lid. Have a strip of muslin or cheese cloth dipped in hot paraffin or suet and quickly bind the seam of the lid. This will remove all danger of salt water entering the pudding. Now cover the mold thoroughly with ice and salt.

Make sure that your packing tub or bucket has a hole below the top of the mold, so that the salt water will be drained off.

If you are packing in small molds, each mold, as fast as it is closed, should be wrapped in wax paper and put down into the salt and ice. These must be filled quickly and packed.

Molds should stand two hours, and may stand longer.

## TO REMOVE ICE CREAMS, ICES AND PUDDINGS FROM MOLDS

Ice cream may be molded in the freezer; you will then have a perfectly round smooth mold, which serves very well for puddings that are to be garnished, and saves a great deal of trouble and extra expense for salt and ice.

As cold water is warmer than the ordinary freezing mixture, after you lift the can or mold, wipe off the salt, hold it for a minute under the cold water spigot, then quickly wipe the top and bottom and remove the lid. Loosen the pudding with a limber knife, hold the mold a little slanting, give it a shake, and nine times out of ten it will come out quickly, having the perfect shape of the can or mold. If the cream still sticks and refuses to come out, wipe the mold with a towel wrung from warm water. Hot water spoils the gloss of puddings, and unless you know exactly how to use it, the cream is too much melted to garnish.

All frozen puddings, water ices, sherbets and sorbets are frozen and molded according to these directions.

The quantities given in these recipes are arranged in equal amounts, so that for a smaller number of persons they can be easily divided.

## QUANTITIES FOR SERVING

Each quart of ice cream will serve, in dessert plates, four persons. In stem ice cream dishes, silver or glass, it will serve six persons. A quart of ice or sherbet will fill ten small sherbet stem glasses, to serve with the meat course at dinner. This quantity will serve in lemonade glasses eight persons.

# Philadelphia Ice Creams

## BURNT ALMOND ICE CREAM

1 quart of cream
½ pound of sugar
4 ounces of sweet almonds
1 tablespoonful of caramel
1 teaspoonful of vanilla extract
4 tablespoonfuls of sherry

Shell, blanch and roast the almonds until they are a golden brown, then grate them. Put half the cream and all the sugar over the fire in a double boiler. Stir until the sugar is dissolved, take it from the fire, add the caramel and the almonds, and, when cold, add the remaining pint of cream, the vanilla and the sherry. Freeze as directed on page 7.

This quantity will serve eight persons.

## APRICOT ICE CREAM

6 ounces of sugar
1 quart of cream
1 can of apricots or
1 quart of fresh apricots

If fresh apricots are used, take an extra quarter of a pound of sugar. Put half the cream and all the sugar over the fire in a double boiler and stir until the sugar is dissolved; take from the fire and, when cold, add the remaining cream. Turn the mixture into the freezer, and, when frozen fairly stiff, add the apricots after having been pressed through a colander. Return the lid, adjust the crank, and turn it slowly for five minutes, then remove the dasher and repack.

This quantity should serve ten persons.

## BANANA ICE CREAM

1 quart of cream
6 large bananas
½ pound of sugar
1 teaspoonful of vanilla

Put half the cream and all the sugar over the fire and stir until the sugar is dissolved; take from the fire, and, when perfectly cold, add the remaining half of the cream. Freeze the mixture, and add the bananas mashed or pressed through a colander. Put on the lid, adjust the crank, and turn until the mixture is frozen rather hard.

This quantity will serve ten persons.

## BISCUIT ICE CREAM

6 wine biscuits
1 quart of cream
½ pound of sugar
1 teaspoonful of vanilla

Grate and sift the biscuits. Scald half the cream and the sugar; when cold, add the remaining cream and the vanilla, and freeze. When frozen, remove the dasher, stir in the powdered biscuits, and repack to ripen.

This quantity will serve six persons.

## APPLE ICE CREAM

4 large tart apples
1 quart of cream
½ pound of sugar
1 tablespoonful of lemon juice

Put half the cream and all the sugar over the fire and stir until the sugar is dissolved. When the mixture is perfectly cold, freeze it and add the lemon juice and the apples, pared and grated. Finish the freezing, and repack to ripen.

The apples must be pared at the last minute and grated into the cream. If they are grated on a dish and allowed to remain in the air they will turn very dark and spoil the color of the cream.

## BROWN BREAD ICE CREAM

3 half inch slices of Boston Brown Bread
1 quart of cream
½ pound of sugar
1 teaspoonful of vanilla or
¼ of a vanilla bean or a teaspoonful of vanilla extract

Dry and toast the bread in the oven, grate or pound it, and put it through an ordinary sieve.

Heat half the cream and all the sugar; take from the fire, add vanilla, and, when cold, add the remaining cream, and freeze. When frozen, remove the dasher, stir in the brown bread, repack and stand aside to ripen.

This quantity will serve six persons.

## CARAMEL ICE CREAM, No. 1

1 quart of cream
½ pound of sugar
1 teaspoonful of vanilla

Put four tablespoonfuls of the sugar in an iron frying pan over a strong fire, shake until the sugar melts, turns brown, smokes and burns; add quickly a half cupful of water; let it boil a minute, take from the fire, and put it, with all the sugar and half the cream, in a double boiler over the fire. Stir until the sugar is dissolved, take from the fire, and, when cold, add the remaining cream and vanilla, and freeze.

This quantity will serve six persons.

## CARAMEL ICE CREAM, No. 2

1 quart of cream
1 pint of milk
½ cupful of brown sugar
½ pound of granulated sugar
2 teaspoonfuls of vanilla

Put the brown sugar in a frying pan over the fire, shake it until it melts, burns and smokes.

Take it from the fire and add two tablespoonfuls of water; heat until the sugar is again melted, put it in a double boiler with the milk and all the sugar, stir until the sugar is dissolved, and stand aside to cool. When cold, add half the cream and the vanilla, and freeze. When frozen sufficiently stiff to remove the dasher, stir in the remaining pint of cream whipped to a stiff froth, repack and stand aside for three hours.

This quantity will serve ten persons.

## BISQUE ICE CREAM

1 quart of cream
¼ pound of almond macaroons
4 kisses
½ pound of sugar
1 slice of stale sponge cake or
2 stale lady fingers
1 teaspoonful of caramel
1 teaspoonful of vanilla
If you use it, 4 tablespoonfuls of sherry

Pound the macaroons, kisses, lady fingers or sponge cake, and put them through a colander. Put half the cream and all the sugar over the fire in a double boiler; when the sugar is dissolved, stand the mixture aside to cool; when cold, add the remaining cream, the caramel, sherry and vanilla. Turn the mixture into the freezer, and, when frozen, add the pounded cakes;

stir the mixture until it is perfectly smooth and well mixed, and repack. Bisque ice cream is better for a three hour stand.

This quantity will serve six persons.

## CHOCOLATE ICE CREAM

1 quart of cream
1 pint of milk
½ pound of sugar
4 ounces of chocolate
1 teaspoonful of vanilla or
¼ of a vanilla bean
¼ of a teaspoonful of cinnamon

Grate the chocolate, put it in a double boiler with the milk; stir until hot, and add the sugar, vanilla, cinnamon and one pint of the cream. When cold, freeze; when frozen, remove the dasher and stir in the remaining pint of the cream whipped to a stiff froth.

This will serve ten persons.

## COFFEE ICE CREAM

1 quart of cream
½ pound of pulverized sugar
4 ounces of so-called Mocha coffee

Grind the Mocha rather coarse, put it in the double boiler with one half the cream, and steep over the fire for at least ten minutes. Strain through a fine muslin or flannel bag, pressing it hard to get out all the strength of the coffee. Add the sugar and stir until dissolved; when cold, add the remaining pint of cream and freeze.

This will serve six persons.

## CURAÇAO ICE CREAM

1 quart of cream
1 wineglassful of curaçao
½ pound of sugar
2 tablespoonfuls of orange blossoms water
Juice of two oranges

Put the sugar and half the cream over the fire in a double boiler. When the sugar is dissolved, take it from the fire, and, when cold, add the curaçao, orange juice and orange blossoms water; add the remaining cream, and freeze.

This will serve six persons.

## GINGER ICE CREAM

1 quart of cream
¼ pound of preserved ginger
½ pound of sugar
1 tablespoonful of lemon juice

Put the ginger through an ordinary meat chopper. Heat the sugar, ginger and half the cream in a double boiler; when the sugar is dissolved, take it from the fire, and, when cold, add the lemon juice and remaining cream, and freeze.

## MARASCHINO ICE CREAM

1 quart of cream
½ pound of sugar
1 orange
2 wineglassfuls of maraschino
2 drops of Angostura Bitters, or ½ teaspoonful of extract of wild cherry

Put the sugar and half the cream in a double boiler, and stir until the sugar is dissolved. When cold, add the remaining cream, the juice of the orange, the bitters or wild cherry, and the maraschino, and freeze.

Serve in parfait glasses to six persons.

## LEMON ICE CREAM

1 quart of cream
9 ounces of powdered sugar
4 tablespoonfuls of lemon juice
Juice of one orange
Grated yellow rind of 3 lemons

Mix the sugar, the grated rind and juice of the lemons, and the orange juice together. Put half the cream in a double boiler over the fire; when scalding hot, stand it aside until perfectly cold; add the remaining half of the cream and freeze it rather hard. Remove the crank and the lid, add the sugar mixture, replace the lid and crank, and turn rapidly for five minutes; repack to ripen.

This will serve six people.

## ORANGE ICE CREAM

1 quart of cream
10 ounces of sugar
Juice of 6 large oranges
Grated rind of one orange

Put the sugar, grated yellow rind of the orange and half the cream in a double boiler over the fire; when the sugar is dissolved, take from the fire, and, when *very cold,* add the remaining cream, and freeze. When frozen rather hard, add the orange juice, refreeze, and pack to ripen.

## PINEAPPLE ICE CREAM

1 quart of cream
12 ounces of sugar
1 large ripe pineapple or
1 pint can of grated pineapple
Juice of one lemon

Put half the cream and half the sugar in a double boiler over the fire; when the sugar is dissolved, stand it aside until cold. Pare and grate the pineapple, add the remaining half of the sugar and stand it aside. When the cream is cold, add the remaining cream, and partly freeze. Then add the lemon juice to the pineapple and add it to the frozen cream; turn the freezer five minutes longer, and repack.

This will serve eight or ten persons.

## GREEN GAGE ICE CREAM

1 quart of cream
4 ounces of sugar
1 pint of preserved green gages, free from syrup

Press the green gages through a sieve. Add the sugar to half the cream, stir it in a double boiler until the sugar is dissolved; when cold, add the remaining cream. When this is partly frozen, stir in the green gage pulp, and finish the freezing as directed on page 7.

If the green gages are colorless, add three or four drops of apple green coloring to the cream before freezing.

## RASPBERRY ICE CREAM

1 quart of cream
1 quart of raspberries
12 ounces of sugar
Juice of one lemon

Mash the raspberries; add half the sugar and the lemon juice. Put the remaining sugar and half the cream in a double boiler; stir until the sugar is dissolved, and stand aside to cool; when cold, add the remaining cream, turn the mixture into the freezer, and stir until partly frozen. Remove the lid and add the mashed raspberries, and stir again for five or ten minutes until the mixture is sufficiently hard to repack.

This will serve eight or ten persons.

## STRAWBERRY ICE CREAM

Make precisely the same as raspberry ice cream, substituting one quart of strawberries for the raspberries.

## PISTACHIO ICE CREAM

1 quart of cream
½ pound of sugar
½ pound of shelled pistachio nuts
1 teaspoonful of almond extract
10 drops of green coloring

Blanch and pound or grate the nuts. Put half the cream and all the sugar in a double boiler; stir until the sugar is dissolved and stand aside to cool; when cold, add the nuts, the flavoring and the remaining cream, mix, add the coloring, and turn into the freezer to freeze.

If green coloring matter is not at hand, a little spinach or parsley may be chopped and rubbed with a small quantity of alcohol.

This quantity will serve six persons.

## VANILLA ICE CREAM

1 quart of cream
½ pound of sugar
1 vanilla bean or two teaspoonfuls of vanilla extract

Put the sugar and half the cream in a double boiler over the fire. Split the vanilla bean, scrape out the seeds and add them to the hot cream, and add the bean broken into pieces. Stir until the sugar is dissolved, and strain through a colander. When this is cold, add the remaining cream and freeze. This should be repacked and given two hours to ripen. Four would be better.

This will serve six persons.

## WALNUT ICE CREAM

1 quart of cream
½ pound of sugar
1 teaspoonful of vanilla
1 teaspoonful of caramel
½ pint of black walnut meats

Put the sugar and half the cream over the fire in a double boiler; when the sugar is dissolved, stand it aside to cool. When cold, add the remaining cream, the walnuts, chopped, and the flavoring, and freeze.

This will serve six persons.

# Neapolitan Creams

In this group we have a set of frozen desserts called by many "ice creams," but which are really frozen custards, flavored. In localities where cream is not accessible, the Neapolitan Creams are far better than milk thickened with cornstarch or gelatin.

### CHOCOLATE

1 pint of cream
1 pint of milk
½ pound of sugar
4 eggs
2 ounces of chocolate
1 small piece of stick cinnamon
1 teaspoonful of vanilla

Put the milk and cinnamon over the fire in a double boiler. Beat the yolks of the eggs and sugar until very light, add the well-beaten whites, and stir this into the hot milk. As soon as the mixture begins to thicken, take it from the fire, add the grated chocolate, and, when cold, add the cream and the vanilla. Freeze and pack as directed on page 7.

This is sufficient to serve ten persons.

## CARAMEL

1 pint of cream
1 pint of milk
½ pound of sugar
4 eggs
3 tablespoonfuls of caramel
1 teaspoonful of vanilla

Beat the yolks of the eggs until creamy and add the sugar; beat until light, and then add the well-beaten whites of the eggs. Put the milk over the fire in a double boiler; when hot, add the eggs, and stir and cook until the mixture begins to thicken. Take from the fire, strain through a fine sieve, add the vanilla and caramel, and, when cold, add the cream, and freeze.

This will serve ten persons.

## COFFEE

1 pint of strong black coffee
1 pint of cream
2 eggs
½ pound of sugar
1 teaspoonful of vanilla

Beat the sugar and the yolks of the eggs until light, add the well-beaten whites, and pour into them the coffee, boiling hot. Stir over the fire for a minute, take from the fire, add the vanilla, and, when cold, add the cream, and freeze.

This will serve eight persons.

## VANILLA

1 pint of cream
1 pint of milk
½ pound of sugar
3 eggs
¼ vanilla bean or a teaspoonful of good extract

Put the milk over the fire in a double boiler, and add the vanilla bean, split. Beat the yolks of the eggs and the sugar until light, add the whites beaten to a stiff froth, and stir into them the hot milk. Return the mixture to the double boiler and cook until it begins to thicken, or will coat a knife blade dipped into it. Take from the fire, strain through a colander, and, when cold, add the cream, and freeze. Repack and stand to ripen for three hours or longer.

This will serve eight persons.

## WALNUT

1 pint of cream
1 pint of milk
2 eggs
½ pint of chopped black walnuts
1 teaspoonful of vanilla
1 teaspoonful of caramel

Beat the yolks of the eggs and the sugar until light; add the well-beaten whites, and then the milk, scalding hot. Stir over the fire in a double boiler until the mixture begins to thicken;

take from the fire and add the vanilla and caramel. When cold, add the walnuts and cream, and freeze.

This will serve eight persons.

## NEAPOLITAN BLOCKS

These are made by putting layers of various kinds and colors of ice creams into a brick mold. Pack and freeze. At serving time, cut into slices crosswise of the brick, and serve each slice on a paper mat.

# Ice Creams from Condensed Milk

These creams are not so good as those made from raw cream, but with care and good flavoring are quite as good as the ordinary Neapolitan Creams.

There is one advantage—condensed milk is not so liable to curdle when mixed with fresh fruits. These recipes will answer also for what is sold under the name of "Evaporated Cream." Use unsweetened milk, or allow for the sugar in the sweetened varieties.

### BANANA

6 large bananas
¼ pound of sugar
1 half pint can of condensed milk
½ cupful of water
Juice of one lemon

Press the bananas through a sieve, and add the lemon juice and sugar. Stand aside a half hour, add milk and water, stir until the sugar is dissolved, and freeze as directed on page 7.

This will serve six persons.

## CARAMEL

¼ cupful of brown sugar
½ cupful of granulated sugar
1 cupful of water
2 half pint cans of condensed milk
1 teaspoonful of vanilla

Put the brown sugar in an iron pan, melt and brown it. When it begins to smoke, add two tablespoonfuls of hot water. Stir until liquid. Pour out the milk, rinse the cans with the water, add the caramel, vanilla and granulated sugar. When the sugar is dissolved, freeze as directed on page 7.

This will serve six persons.

## COCOANUT

2 large cocoanuts
1 pint of boiling water
½ pint can of sweetened condensed milk

Grate the cocoanuts and pour over them the boiling water. Stir until it is cool, and press in a sieve. Put the fibre in a cheese cloth and wring it dry; add this to the water that was strained through the sieve. When cold, add condensed milk, and freeze as directed on page 7.

This will serve eight persons.

## CHOCOLATE, No. 1

2 ounces of Baker's chocolate
½ pint of water
1 saltspoonful of ground cinnamon
2 half pint cans of condensed milk
1 teaspoonful of vanilla
¼ pound of sugar

Put the water, chocolate, sugar and cinnamon in a saucepan; stir until boiling. Take from the fire, add the vanilla and the condensed milk. When cold, freeze as directed on page 7.

This will serve six persons.

## CHOCOLATE, No. 2

4 ounces of Baker's chocolate
½ pint of water
½ pound of sugar
2 half pint cans of condensed milk
1 pint of milk
2 teaspoonfuls of vanilla
1 saltspoonful of ground cinnamon

Put the chocolate, sugar, water and cinnamon in a saucepan over the fire. Stir until the mixture boils. Take from the fire, and add all the remaining ingredients. When cold, freeze as directed on page 7.

This will serve eight persons.

## COFFEE

1 pint of strong black coffee
½ cupful of sugar
½ pint can of condensed milk
1 teaspoonful of vanilla

Add the sugar to the hot coffee, and stir until it is dissolved; add the milk, using water enough to rinse out the cans; add the vanilla. When the mixture is cold, freeze, turning it rapidly toward the end of the freezing.

This will serve four persons.

## PEACH

12 ripe or canned peaches
4 peach kernels
½ pint of water
2 half pint cans of unsweetened condensed milk
½ pound of sugar

Put the sugar, water and peach kernels over the fire; stir until the sugar is dissolved, and boil three minutes. Pare the peaches and press them through a colander, add to them the strained syrup. When cold, turn the mixture into the freezer and turn the crank slowly until partly frozen; add the milk, and continue the freezing.

Omit the water and use less sugar with canned peaches.

This will serve ten persons.

## ORANGE, No. 1

1 full pint of orange juice
2/3 cupful of sugar
½ pint can of condensed milk
Grated yellow rind of two oranges

Grate the rinds into the sugar, add milk and enough water to rinse cans. When sugar is dissolved, stand it in a cold place. Put orange juice in the freezer and freeze it quite hard; add sweetened milk, and freeze again quickly.

This will serve four persons.

## ORANGE, No. 2

Freeze a full quart of orange juice. When quite hard, add a can of sweetened condensed milk, freeze it again, and serve at once.

This is very nice and will serve eight persons.

## ORANGE GELATIN CREAM

½ pint of orange juice
1 package of orange Jello
½ pound of sugar
1 pint can of unsweetened condensed milk
½ pint of water

Add the grated yellow rind of two oranges to the Jello; add the sugar and the water, boiling. Stir until the sugar and Jello are dissolved, add the orange juice, and when the mixture is cold, put it in the freezer and stir slowly until it begins to freeze. Add the condensed milk, and continue the freezing.

This is nice served in tall glasses, with the beaten whites of the eggs made into a meringue and heaped on top.

In this way it will serve eight persons.

## SOUR SOP

1 large sour sop
¼ pound of sugar
½ pint can of unsweetened condensed milk
4 tablespoonfuls of boiling water
Juice of one lime

Squeeze the sour sop, which should measure nearly one quart; add the sugar melted in the water with the lime juice and milk, and freeze slowly.

This will serve ten persons.

# Frozen Puddings and Desserts

## ALASKA BAKE

Make a vanilla ice cream, one or two quarts, as the occasion demands. When the ice cream is frozen, pack it in a brick mold, cover each side of the mold with letter paper and fasten the bottom and lid. Wrap the whole in wax paper and pack it in salt and ice; freeze for at least two hours before serving time. At serving time, make a meringue from the whites of six eggs beaten to a froth; add six tablespoonfuls of sifted powdered sugar and beat until fine and dry. Turn the ice cream from the mold, place it on a serving platter, and stand the platter on a steak board or an ordinary thick plank. Cover the mold with the meringue pressed through a star tube in a pastry bag, or spread it all over the ice cream as you would ice a cake. Decorate the top quickly, and dust it thickly with powdered sugar; stand it under the gas burners in a gas broiler or on the grate in a hot coal or wood oven until it is lightly browned, and send it quickly to the table. There is no danger of the ice cream melting if you will protect the under side of the plate.

The meringue acts as a nonconductor for the upper part.

A two quart mold with meringue will serve ten persons.

### ALEXANDER BOMB

1 pint of cream
1 pint of milk
4 eggs
4 tart apples
1 pint of water
1 glassful of orange blossoms water
1 wineglassful of curaçao
1 pound of sugar
Juice of one lemon

Peel, core and quarter the apples; put them in a saucepan with the grated yellow rind of the lemon, half the sugar and all the water; boil until tender, and add the juice of the lemon; rub the apples through a sieve. When cold, freeze. Whip the cream. Beat the eggs and the remaining sugar and add them to the milk, hot; stir until the mixture thickens, take from the fire, and, when cold, add the orange blossoms water and the curaçao; freeze in another freezer. Divide the whipped cream, and stir one-half into the first and one-half into the other mixture. Line a melon mold with the custard mixture, fill the centre space with the frozen apples, and cover over another layer of the custard; put over a sheet of letter paper and put on the lid. Bind the seam with a strip of muslin dipped in paraffin or suet, and pack the mold in salt and ice; freeze for at least two hours. Serve plain, or it may be garnished with whipped cream.

This will serve twelve persons.

## BISCUITS AMERICANA

1 quart of cream
½ pound of sugar
¼ pound of Jordan almonds
1 teaspoonful of almond extract
1 teaspoonful of vanilla
Yolks of six eggs
Grated rind of one lemon

Put half the cream in a double boiler over the fire, and, when hot, add the yolks of the eggs and sugar, beaten until very, very light; add all the flavoring, and stand aside until very cold; when cold, freeze in an ordinary freezer. Whip the remaining pint of cream, add one-half of it to the frozen mixture, repack and stand aside to ripen. Blanch, dry and chop the almonds. Put them in the oven and shake constantly until they are a golden brown. At serving time, fill the frozen mixture quickly into paper cases; have the remaining whipped cream in a pastry bag with star tube, make a little rosette on the top of each case, dust thickly with the chopped almonds, and send to the table.

This will fill twelve cases of ordinary size.

## BISCUITS GLACÉS

1 pint of cream
¾ pound of sugar
1 pint of water
1 gill of sherry
2 tablespoonfuls of brandy
1 teaspoonful of vanilla
Yolks of six eggs

Put the sugar and water in a saucepan over the fire and stir until the sugar is dissolved; wipe down the sides of the pan, and boil until the syrup spins a heavy thread or makes a soft ball when dropped into cold water. Beat the yolks of the eggs to a cream, add them to the boiling syrup, and with an egg beater whisk over the fire until you have a custard-like mixture that will thickly coat a knife blade; strain through a sieve into a bowl, and whisk until the mixture is stiff and cold. It should look like a very light sponge cake batter. Add the flavoring. Whip the cream and stir it carefully into the mixture. Fill the mixture into paper cases or individual dishes, stand them in a freezing cave or in a tin bucket that is well packed in salt and ice, cover and freeze for at least four or five hours.

If you do not have a freezing cave, pack a good sized tin kettle in a small tub or water bucket. The kettle must have a tight fitting lid. Stand your cases or molds on the bottom of the tin kettle, which is packed in salt and ice. Put on top a sheet of letter paper, on top of this another layer of molds or cases, and so continue until you have the kettle filled. Put the lid on the kettle and cover with salt and ice. Make sure that you have a hole half-way up in the packing bucket or tub, so that there is no danger of salt water overflowing the kettle. This is a homely but very good freezing cave.

At serving time, dust the tops of the biscuits with grated macaroons or chopped almonds, dish on paper mats, and send to the table.

This will fill fifteen biscuit cases.

## BISCUITS à la MARIE

½ pound of sugar
1 pint of water
½ pint of cream
½ pound of almond macaroons
¼ pound of candied or Maraschino cherries
1 teaspoonful of bitter almond extract
Yolks of six eggs

Boil the sugar and water until the syrup will spin a heavy thread. Add the eggs, beaten until very light. Whip this over the fire for three minutes, take it from the fire, strain into a bowl, and whip until thick and cold. Add the flavoring and the macaroons, that have been dried, grated and sifted. Add the cream, whipped. Fill the mixture into paper cases, and freeze as directed for Biscuits Glacés.

An extra half pint of cream may be whipped for garnish at serving time, if desired; otherwise, garnish the top with chopped maraschino cherries, and send to the table.

This will fill twelve biscuit cases.

## BOMB GLACÉ

Pack a two quart bomb glacé mold in salt and ice. Remove the lid, and line the mold with a quart of well-made vanilla ice cream. Fill the centre with one half the recipe for Biscuit Glacé mixture, that has been packed in a freezer until icy cold. Put on the lid, bind the edge with a piece of muslin dipped in paraffin or suet, cover the mold with salt and ice, and stand aside three hours to freeze.

This will serve twelve persons.

## BISCUIT TORTONI

1 quart of cream
½ pound of sugar
1 gill of maraschino
2 tablespoonfuls of sherry
1 teaspoonful of vanilla
Yolks of six eggs

Put half the cream in a double boiler over the fire. Beat the sugar and yolks together until very, very light, add them to the hot cream and stir over the fire until the mixture begins to thicken. Take from the fire, and, when very cold, add the vanilla, maraschino and sherry, and freeze. When frozen, stir in the remaining cream, whipped to a stiff froth. Fill individual dishes or paper cases, stand at once in the freezing kettle or ice cave; pack and freeze from three to four hours.

This will fill twelve cases.

## CABINET PUDDING, ICED

1 quart of milk
6 eggs
¼ pound of powdered sugar
1 tablespoonful of powdered gelatin
¼ pound of macaroons and lady fingers, mixed
½ pound of conserved cherries or pineapple
½ pound of stale sponge cake

Grate the macaroons and lady fingers, and rub them through a coarse sieve. Cut the sponge cake into slices and then into strips. Put the milk over the fire in a double boiler and add the eggs and sugar beaten together until light; stir and cook until the mixture is sufficiently thick to coat a knife blade. Take from the fire, add the gelatin, strain, and stand it aside to cool. Garnish the bottom of a two quart melon mold with the cherries or pineapple, put in a layer of the sponge cake, then a sprinkling of the macaroons and lady fingers, another layer of the cherries, then the sponge cake, and so continue until you have all the ingredients used. Add a teaspoonful of vanilla to the custard, pour it in the mold, cover the mold with the lid, bind the seam with muslin dipped in paraffin or suet, pack in salt and ice, and stand aside for three hours.

At serving time, dip the mold quickly into hot water, wipe it off, remove the lid and turn the pudding on to a cold platter. Pour around a well-made Montrose Sauce, and send to the table.

This will serve ten or twelve persons.

## ICED CAKE

Make an Angel Food or a Sunshine Cake and bake it in a square mold. Make a plain frozen custard, and flavor it with vanilla; pack it and stand it aside until serving time. Cut off the top of the cake, take out the centre, leaving a bottom and wall one inch thick. At serving time, fill the cake quickly with the frozen custard, replace the top, dust it thickly with powdered sugar and chopped almonds, and send it to the table with a sauceboat of cold Montrose Sauce.

This cake may be varied by using different garnishings. Maraschino cherries may be used in place of almonds, or the base of the cake may be garnished with preserved green walnuts or green gages, or the top and sides may be garnished with rosettes of whipped cream.

This will serve twelve persons.

## QUICK CARAMEL PARFAIT

Make a quart of Caramel Ice Cream, pack, and stand it aside for two hours. At serving time, stir in a pint of cream, whipped to a stiff froth, dish in parfait glasses, and send to the table. The top of the glasses may be garnished with whipped cream, if desired.

This will fill eight glasses.

## QUICK CAFÉ PARFAIT

Make a quart of plain Coffee Ice Cream, freeze and pack it. Whip one pint of cream. At serving time, stir the whipped cream into the frozen coffee cream, dish it at once into tall parfait glasses, garnish the top with a rosette of whipped cream, and send at once to the table.

This will fill eight glasses.

## QUICK STRAWBERRY PARFAIT

This is made precisely the same as other parfaits, with Strawberry Ice Cream, and whipped cream stirred in at serving time. Serve in parfait glasses, garnish the top with whipped cream, with a strawberry in the centre on top.

This will fill eight glasses.

## QUICK CHOCOLATE PARFAIT

Make one quart of Chocolate Ice Cream, and add one pint of whipped cream, according to the preceding recipes.

This will serve eight persons.

## MONTE CARLO PUDDING

1 quart of cream
6 ounces of sugar (2/3 of a cupful)
4 tablespoonfuls of creme de violette
½ pound of candied violets
1 teaspoonful of vanilla

Put half the cream over the fire in a double boiler. Pound or roll the violets, sift them, add the sugar and sufficient hot cream to dissolve them. Take the cream from the fire, add the violet sugar, and stir until it is dissolved; when cold, add the flavoring and the remaining cream. Freeze, and pack into a two quart pyramid mold; pack in salt and ice for at least two hours. At serving time, turn the ice on to a platter, garnish the base with whipped cream, and the whole with candied violets.

This will serve six to eight persons.

## BOSTON PUDDING

Make Boston Brown Bread Ice Cream and half the recipe for Tutti Frutti. When both are frozen, line a melon mold with the Brown Bread Ice Cream, fill the centre with the Tutti Frutti, cover over more of the Brown Bread Ice Cream, fasten tightly, and bind the seam of the lid with a strip of muslin dipped in paraffin or suet. Pack in salt and ice for at least two hours. At serving time, dip the mold quickly into hot water, turn the pudding on to a cold platter, pour around the base caramel sauce, and serve at once.

This will serve twelve persons.

## MONTROSE PUDDING

1 quart of cream
1 cupful of granulated sugar
1 tablespoonful of vanilla
1 pint of strawberry water ice
Yolks of six eggs

Put half the cream over the fire in a double boiler. Beat the yolks and sugar together until light, add them to the boiling cream, and cook and stir for one minute until it begins to thicken. Take from the fire, add the remaining pint of cream and the vanilla, and stand aside until very cold. Freeze, and pack into a round or melon mold, leaving a well in the centre. Fill this well with Strawberry Water Ice that has been frozen an hour before, and cover it with some of the pudding mixture that you have left in the freezer. Fasten the lid, bind the seam with a piece of muslin dipped in suet or paraffin, and pack in salt and ice to stand for not less than two hours, four is better. Serve with Montrose Sauce poured around it.

This will serve twelve persons.

## NESSELRODE PUDDING

1 pint of Spanish chestnuts
½ pound of sugar
1 pint of boiling water
½ pint of shelled almonds
1 pound of French candied fruit, mixed
1 pint of heavy cream
¼ pound of candied pineapple
Yolks of six eggs

Shell the chestnuts, scald and remove the brown skins, cover with boiling water and boil until they are tender, not too soft, and press them through a sieve. Shell, blanch and pound the almonds. Cut the fruit into tiny pieces. Put the sugar and water in a saucepan, stir until the sugar is dissolved, wipe down the sides of the pan, and boil without stirring until the syrup forms a soft ball when dropped into ice water.

Beat the yolks of the eggs until very light, add them to the boiling syrup, and stir over the fire until the mixture again boils; take it from the fire, and with an ordinary egg beater, whisk the mixture until it is cold and thick as sponge cake batter. Add the fruit, the chestnuts, almond paste, a teaspoonful of vanilla and, if you use it, four tablespoonfuls of sherry. Turn the mixture into the freezer, and, when it is frozen, stir in the cream whipped to a stiff froth. The mixture may now be repacked in the can, or it may be put into small molds or one large mold, and re-packed for ripening.

If packed in a large mold, this will serve fifteen persons; in the small molds or paper cases, it will serve eighteen persons.

## NESSELRODE PUDDING, AMERICANA

1 small bottle, or sixteen preserved marrons
1 quart of cream
4 ounces of sugar
4 tablespoonfuls of sherry
1 tablespoonful of vanilla
Yolks of six eggs

Put half the cream in a double boiler over the fire; when hot, add the eggs and sugar beaten until light. Cook a minute, and cool. When cold, add one small bottle of marrons broken into quarters and the syrup from the bottle, the sherry and vanilla. Freeze, stirring slowly. When frozen, stir in the remaining cream whipped to a stiff froth. Pack in small molds in salt and ice as directed. These should freeze three hours at least.

This will make twelve small molds.

## ORANGE SOUFFLE

1 quart of cream
1 pint of orange juice
½ box of gelatin
¾ pound of sugar
Yolks of six eggs

Cover the gelatin with a half cupful of cold water and soak for a half hour. Add a half cupful of boiling water, stir until the gelatin is dissolved, and add the sugar and the orange juice. Beat the yolks of the eggs until very light. Whip the cream. Add the uncooked yolks to the orange mixture, strain in the gelatin, stand the bowl in cold water and stir slowly until the mixture begins to thicken; stir in carefully the whipped cream, turn it in a mold or an ice cream freezer, pack with salt and ice, and stand aside three hours to freeze. This should not be frozen as hard as ice cream, and must not be stirred while freezing. Make sure, however, that the gelatin is thoroughly mixed with the other ingredients before putting the mixture into the freezer.

This will serve twelve people.

By changing the flavoring, using lemon in the place of orange, or a pint of strawberry juice, or a pint of raspberry and currant juice, an endless variety of soufflés may be made from this same recipe. These may be served plain, or with Montrose Sauce.

## PLOMBIERE

1 quart of cream
½ pound of Jordan almonds
½ pound of sugar
½ pound of Sultana raisins
Yolks of six eggs

Blanch the almonds and pound them to a paste, or use a half pound of ordinary almond paste. Put half the cream in a double boiler over the fire, add the yolks and sugar beaten to a cream, add the almond paste. Stir until the mixture begins to thicken, take from the fire and beat with an egg beater for three minutes. Strain through a fine sieve, and, when very cold, add the Sultanas and the remaining cream. Freeze, turning the dasher very slowly at first and more rapidly toward the end. Remove the dasher, scrape down the sides of the can and pull the cream up, making a well in the centre. Fill this well half full with apricot jam, cover over the pudding mixture, making it smooth; repack, and stand aside for two hours.

Serve plain or with a cold Purée of Apricots. This will serve twelve persons.

## QUEEN PUDDING

Make a Strawberry Water Ice or Frozen Strawberries. Pack a three quart mold in a bucket or tub of ice and salt. Line the mold with the Strawberry Ice, fill the centre with Tutti Frutti, using half recipe; put on the lid, bind the seam, and stand aside for at least two hours. When ready to serve, turn the pudding from the mold into the centre of a large round dish, garnish the base with whipped cream pressed through a star tube, and garnish the pudding with candied cherries. Here and there around the base of the whipped cream place a marron glacé.

This will serve fifteen persons.

## ICE CREAM CROQUETTES

Mold vanilla ice cream with the ordinary pyramid ice cream spoon, roll them quickly in grated macaroons, and serve on a paper mat.

## ICED RICE PUDDING WITH A COMPOTE OF ORANGES

### For the Pudding

½ cupful of rice
1 quart of cream
1 pint of milk
2 teaspoonfuls of vanilla extract or
½ vanilla bean
½ pound of sugar
Yolks of six eggs

Rub the rice in a dry towel, and put it over the fire in a pint of cold water. Bring to a boil and boil twenty minutes; drain, add the milk and cook it in a double boiler a half hour. While this is boiling, whip the cream to a stiff froth, and stand it in a cold place until wanted. Press the rice through a fine sieve and return it to the double boiler. Beat the yolks of the eggs and the sugar until light, stir them into the hot rice, and stir and cook about two minutes, until the mixture begins to thicken. Take from the fire, add the vanilla, and stand aside until very cold. When cold, freeze, turning the dasher rapidly toward the last. Remove the dasher and stir in the whipped cream. Scrape down the sides of the can, and smooth the pudding. Put on the lid, fasten the hole in the top with a cork, put over the top a piece of waxed paper, and pack with salt and ice. Stand aside for at least two or three hours. Be very careful that the hole in the tub is open, to prevent the salt water from overflowing the can.

### For the Compote

1 dozen nice oranges
1 pound of sugar
½ cupful of water
1 teaspoonful of lemon juice

Put the sugar and water over the fire to boil, wipe down the sides of the pan, skim the syrup, add the lemon juice, and boil until it spins a thread. Peel the oranges, cut them into halves crosswise, and with a sharp knife remove the cores. Dip one piece at a time into the hot syrup and place them on a platter to cool. Pour over any syrup that may be left.

This syrup must be thick, but not sufficiently thick to harden on the oranges.

To dish the pudding, lift the can from the ice, wipe it carefully on the outside, wrap the bottom of the mold in a towel dipped in boiling water, or hold it half an instant under the cold water spigot. Then with a limber knife or spatula loosen the pudding from the side of the can and shake it out into the centre of a large round plate. Heap the oranges on top of the pudding, making them in a pyramid, put the remaining quantity around the base of the pudding, pour over the syrup and send to the table.

This pudding sounds elaborate and troublesome, but it is exceedingly palatable and one of the handsomest of all frozen dishes.

This will serve twenty persons. In ice cream stem dishes it will serve twenty-four persons.

## SULTANA ROLL

1½ quarts of cream
½ pound of granulated sugar
½ cupful of Sultanas
4 tablespoonfuls of sherry
2 ounces of shelled pistachio nuts
1 teaspoonful of almond extract
10 drops of green coloring

Put one pint of cream and the sugar over the fire in a double boiler, and stir until the sugar is dissolved; take from the fire, and, when cold, add a pint of the remaining cream. Chop the pistachio nuts very fine or put them through the meat grinder, add them to the cream and add the flavoring and coloring, and freeze. Whip the remaining pint of cream to a stiff froth. Sprinkle the Sultanas with sherry and let them stand while you are freezing the pudding. When the pudding is frozen, remove the dasher and line a long round mold with the pistachio cream. If nothing better is at hand, use pound baking powder cans, and line them to the depth of one inch. Add the Sultanas to the whipped cream and stir in two tablespoonfuls of powdered sugar. Fill the spaces in the cans with the whipped cream mixture, and put another layer of the pistachio cream over the top. Put on the lids, wrap each can in waxed paper, and put them down into coarse salt and ice, to freeze for at least two hours. At serving time, turn the puddings on to a long platter, fill the bottom of the platter with Claret or Strawberry Sauce, and send to the table.

This quantity cut into half inch slices will serve twelve persons.

## SULTANA PUDDING

1 pint of milk
1 pint of cream
6 ounces of sugar
1 cupful of Sultanas
1 teaspoonful of vanilla
4 tablespoonfuls of sherry (if you use it)
Yolks of four eggs

Put the milk in a double boiler, and, when hot, add the yolks and sugar beaten together; stir until this begins to thicken. Take from the fire, add the vanilla, and, when cold, freeze it. Put the sherry over the Sultanas. Garnish the bottom of a melon mold with the Sultanas, pack it in coarse ice and salt ready for the frozen pudding. Remove the dasher from the frozen mixture, and stir in the cream that has been whipped to a stiff froth. Add the remainder of the Sultanas and pack at once into the mold; put on the lid and fasten as directed in other recipes.

This may be served plain or with whipped cream garnished with Sultanas.

This will serve eight persons.

## THE MERRY WIDOW

Dish a pyramid of vanilla ice cream into a stem individual ice cream glass. Garnish the base of the ice cream with fresh strawberries, dust the cream thickly with toasted piñon nuts, and baste the whole with four tablespoonfuls of Claret Sauce flavored with two tablespoonfuls of rum.

## TUTTI FRUTTI PUDDING

1 pint of milk
1 pint of cream
½ pint of mixed candied fruits
4 eggs
1 cupful of sugar
1 teaspoonful of vanilla
2 tablespoonfuls of sherry
1 tablespoonful of brandy

Put the milk over the fire in a double boiler, add the yolks of the eggs and the sugar beaten together until light. When the mixture begins to thicken, take it from the fire and stand it aside until perfectly cold. Add all the flavorings. When the mixture is cold, add the cream, and partly freeze it; then add the fruit, and freeze to the right consistency. This should be packed at least two hours to ripen.

This will serve eight persons.

## TUTTI FRUTTI, ITALIAN FASHION

½ pound of sugar
1 pint of water
1 pint of cream
½ pint of chopped mixed candied fruits
1 teaspoonful of vanilla
4 tablespoonfuls of sherry
Yolks of six eggs

Pour the sherry over the fruit. Beat the yolks until creamy. Put the sugar and water over the fire, stir until the sugar is dissolved, and boil five minutes; add the yolks of the eggs, beat until it again reaches the boiling point, take from the fire and beat until cold and thick. Add the cream, the fruit and the vanilla. Freeze as directed on page 7.

This is usually served in small ice cream glasses garnished with whipped cream, or may be served plain. In the absence of ice cream glasses, use ordinary punch glasses.

This will fill ten glasses.

## LALLA ROOKH

Fill a lemonade or ice cream glass two-thirds full of vanilla ice cream. Make a little well in the centre and fill the space with rum and sherry mixed. Allow four tablespoonfuls of rum and six of sherry to each half dozen cups.

## PEACHES MELBA

Dish a helping of vanilla ice cream in the centre of the serving plate, place in the centre of the ice cream a whole brandied peach, press it down into the ice cream, baste over four tablespoonfuls of Claret Sauce, and serve.

## LILLIAN RUSSELL

Cut into halves small very cold cantaloupes. Remove the seeds; fill the centres of the half melons with vanilla ice cream, and garnish with whipped cream pressed through a small star tube. Dish the halves on paper mats on a dessert plate, and send to the table.

## ARROWROOT CREAM

1 quart of milk
6 ounces of sugar
1 level tablespoonful of arrowroot
2 teaspoonfuls of vanilla

Moisten the arrowroot with a little cold milk; put the remaining milk in a double boiler; when hot, add the arrowroot and cook ten minutes; add the sugar, take from the fire, and add the vanilla. When perfectly cold, freeze as directed on page 7.

This will serve six persons.

## ENGLISH APRICOT CREAM

½ pint of apricot jam
1 pint of cream
½ pint of milk
2 tablespoonfuls of noyau
Juice of one lemon

Mix the jam and the cream, then carefully add the noyau and the lemon juice. Press through a fine sieve, add the milk, and freeze as directed on page 7.

This will serve six persons.

## FROZEN CUSTARD

1 quart of milk
6 ounces of sugar
2 teaspoonfuls of vanilla
Yolks of four eggs

Put the milk in a double boiler, add the yolks of the eggs and the sugar beaten together, and stir until the mixture thickens. Take from the fire, and, when cold, add the vanilla. Turn into the freezer and freeze as directed. A little chopped conserved fruit may be added at last when the dasher is removed. Chopped black walnuts may also be added.

This will serve six persons.

## GELATIN ICE CREAM

1 quart of milk
½ pint of cream
6 ounces of sugar
1 tablespoonful of granulated gelatin
2 teaspoonfuls of vanilla

Cover the gelatin with a little cold milk and stand it aside for fifteen minutes. Put the remaining milk in a double boiler; when scalding hot, add the sugar and the gelatin; stir until the sugar is dissolved, take from the fire, and, when perfectly cold, add the cream and the vanilla. Freeze as directed on page 7.

This will serve six persons.

## FROZEN PLUM PUDDING

2 pint cans of condensed milk
½ cupful of seeded raisins
½ pound of sugar
24 almonds that have been blanched and chopped
2 ounces of shredded citron
¼ pound of candied cherries
2 teaspoonfuls of vanilla
2 tablespoonfuls of sherry
½ pint of water
Yolks of four eggs

Put milk in a double boiler over the fire, and stir until the milk is thoroughly heated; add the yolks of the eggs and the sugar beaten together, cook until it begins to thicken, take from the fire and strain. When cold, add the citron, raisins, the cherries cut into quarters, the almonds, vanilla and sherry. When this is perfectly cold, freeze as directed. Do not repack or allow the mixture to stand in the freezer more than a half hour.

Serve plain or with Montrose Sauce.

One quart of good rich milk may be used in place of the condensed milk.

This will serve twelve persons.

## CHARLOTTE GLACÉ

Make a quart of vanilla ice cream and stir into it a pint of cream whipped to a stiff froth. Line round stiff paper charlotte boxes with lady fingers, fill them with the iced mixture, and place them at once in a can or bucket packed in salt and ice to freeze for one or two hours.

This quantity will fill twelve boxes.

## MAPLE PANACHÉE

Fill stem ice cream dishes half full with caramel ice cream; on top put a layer of vanilla ice cream. Smooth it down and dust thickly with toasted pecan nuts chopped fine.

A pint of each cream will fill six dishes.

## GERMAN CHERRY BISCUITS

Fill paper cases half full of pineapple water ice. Put over a layer of candied cherries chopped, then a layer of vanilla ice cream; smooth it quickly, place a marron glacé in the centre, and garnish the cream with a meringue made from the whites of two eggs and two tablespoonfuls of powdered sugar. Dust this with grated macaroons, and send to the table. Make the meringue and grate the macaroons before dishing the ice cream.

A pint of each cream will fill eight cases.

## FRUIT SALAD, ICED

Make one quart of lemon or orange water ice and stand it aside for at least one or two hours to ripen. Make a fruit salad from stemmed strawberries, sliced bananas cut into tiny bits, a few very ripe cherries, a grated pineapple if you have it, and the pulp of four or five oranges. After the water ice is frozen rather hard, pack it in a border mold, put on the lid or cover and bind the seam with a strip of muslin dipped in paraffin or suet, and repack to freeze for three or four hours. Sweeten the fruit combination, if you like, add a tablespoonful or two of brandy and sherry, and stand this on the ice until *very cold*. At serving time, turn the mold of water ice on to a round compote dish, quickly fill the centre with fruit salad, garnish the outside with fresh roses or violets, and send at once to the table.

This will serve eight or ten persons at luncheon.

## COUPE ST. JACQUE

Make a fruit salad as in preceding recipe. Make a pint of orange or strawberry ice. At serving time fill parfait or ice cream glasses half full of the fruit salad, fill the remaining half with water ice, smooth it over, garnish the top with whipped cream, put a maraschino cherry in the centre, and serve. Other fruits may be used for the salad.

This should make twelve tumblers.

# Water Ices and Sherbets or Sorbets

A water ice is a mixture of water, fruit and sugar, frozen without much stirring; in fact, a water ice can be made in an ordinary tin kettle packed in a bucket. If an ice cream freezer is used, the stirring should be done occasionally. Personally, I prefer to pack the can, put on the lid and fasten the hole with a cork rather than to use the dasher, stirring now and then with a paddle. If you use the crank, turn slowly for a few minutes, then allow the mixture to stand for five minutes; turn slowly again, and again rest, and continue this until the water ice is frozen. A much longer time is required for freezing water ice than ice cream.

When the mixture is thoroughly frozen, take out the dasher, scrape down the sides of the can, give the ice a thorough beating with a wooden spoon; put the cork in the lid of the can, draw the water from the tub, repack it with coarse ice and salt, cover it with paper and a piece of blanket or burlap, and stand aside for two or three hours to ripen just as you would ice cream.

When it is necessary to make water ice every day or two, it is best to make a syrup and stand it aside ready for use.

Fruit jellies may be used in the place of fresh fruits, allowing one pint of jelly, the juice of one lemon and a half pound of sugar to each quart of water.

When water ice is correctly frozen, it has the appearance of hard wet snow. It must not be frothy nor light.

A sherbet or sorbet is made from the same mixture as a water ice, stirred constantly while it is freezing, and has a meringue, made from the white of one egg and a tablespoonful of powdered sugar, stirred in after the dasher is removed.

## APPLE ICE

1 pound of tart apples
1 cupful of sugar
1 pint of water
Juice of one lemon or lime

Quarter and core the apples, but do not pare them. Slice them, add the water, cover and stew until tender, about five minutes. Press through a sieve, add the sugar and lemon juice. When cold, freeze as directed. Serve in lemonade glasses at dinner with roasted duck, goose or pork.

This will serve six persons.

## APRICOT ICE

1 quart can of apricots
½ cupful of sugar
1 pint of water
Juice of one lemon

Press the apricots through a sieve, add all the other ingredients, and serve. This is nice served in lemonade glasses for afternoon tea. Pass sweet wafers.

This will serve eight persons.

## CHERRY ICE

2 full quarts of sour cherries
1 pound of sugar
1 quart of water

Stew the cherries in the water for ten minutes and press through a sieve, add the sugar, and, if you have it, two drops of Angostura Bitters; when cold, freeze it as directed on page 63.

This will serve ten persons.

## CURRANT WATER ICE

1 pint of currant juice
1 pound of sugar
1 pint of boiling water

Add the sugar to the water, and stir over the fire until it is dissolved. Boil five minutes, take from the fire; when cool, add the currant juice. When cold, freeze as directed on page 63.

This will serve six persons.

## CURRANT AND RASPBERRY WATER ICE

1 pint of currant juice
1 pint of raspberry juice
1 pint of water
¾ pound of sugar

Add the sugar to the water, stir until boiling, boil five minutes, and, when cool, add the raspberry and currant juices, and freeze as directed.

This will serve six persons; in punch glasses, eight persons.

## GRAPE WATER ICE

1 pint of grape juice
1 quart of water
1 pound of sugar
Juice of one lemon

Boil the sugar and water together for five minutes, take from the fire, add the lemon juice, and skim. When cold, add the grape juice, and freeze as directed.

If fresh grapes are to be used, select Muscatels or Concords. Pulp the grapes, boil the pulps, press them through a sieve, and add the skins and the pulps to the sugar and water. Boil five minutes, press as much as possible through a sieve, and freeze.

This will serve eight persons.

## LEMON WATER ICE

4 large lemons
1 quart of water
1¼ pounds of sugar

Grate the yellow rind of two lemons into the sugar, add the water, stir over the fire until the sugar is dissolved, and boil for five minutes. Strain, and stand aside to cool. When cold, add the juice of the lemons, and freeze as directed on page 63.

This will serve six persons.

## GINGER WATER ICE

6 ounces of preserved ginger
4 lemons
1 quart of water
1 pound of sugar

Put four ounces of the ginger through an ordinary meat grinder, and cut the remaining two ounces into fine bits. Boil the sugar and water together for five minutes, and add the lemon juice and ground ginger. Take from the fire, add the bits of ginger, and, when cold, freeze as directed. Ginger water ice is better for a two hour stand, after it is frozen. Nice to serve with roasted or braised beef.

This will serve six persons; in small punch glasses, eight.

## MILLE FRUIT WATER ICE

½ pint of grape juice
6 lemons
1 orange
4 tablespoonfuls of sherry
½ pound of preserved cherries or pineapple, or both mixed
1½ pounds of sugar
1 quart of water

Grate the yellow rind of the orange and one lemon into the sugar, add the water, stir over the fire until the sugar is dissolved, boil five minutes, and strain. Add the fruit cut into small pieces, the juice of the orange and the lemons; when cold, add the grape juice and sherry, and freeze, using the dasher. Do not stir rapidly, but stir continuously, as slowly as possible. When the mixture is frozen, remove the dasher and repack the can; ripen at least two hours.

This is one of the nicest of all the water ices, and may be served on the top of Coupe St. Jacque, or at dinner in sherbet glasses with roasted veal or beef.

This will serve ten persons.

## ORANGE WATER ICE

12 large oranges
1 pound of sugar
1 quart of water

Grate the yellow rind from three oranges into the sugar, add the water, boil five minutes, and strain; when cold, add the orange juice, and freeze as directed for water ices.

This will serve ten persons.

## POMEGRANATE WATER ICE

12 good sized pomegranates
1 pint of water
1 pound of sugar

Cut the pomegranates into halves, remove the seeds carefully from the inside bitter skin; press them with a potato masher in the colander, allowing the juice to run through into a bowl; be careful not to mash the seeds. Add the sugar to the juice and stir until it is dissolved; then add the water, cold, and freeze.

This is very nice to serve with a meat course, and also nice for the garnish of a fruit salad.

This will serve six persons.

## PINEAPPLE WATER ICE

2 ripe pineapples or
1 quart can of grated pineapple
1 quart of water
1½ pounds of sugar
Juice of two lemons

Pare the pineapples, remove the eyes, and grate the fruit into the water. Add the sugar and lemon juice, boil five minutes, and, when cold, freeze as directed on page 63.

This will serve ten persons.

## STRAWBERRY WATER ICE

1 quart of strawberries
1 pound of sugar
1 quart of water
Juice of two lemons

Add the sugar and the lemon juice to the stemmed strawberries, let them stand one hour; mash them through a colander, and then, if you like, strain through a fine sieve. Add the water, and freeze as directed on page 63.

This will serve eight persons.

## RASPBERRY WATER ICE

1 quart of red raspberries
1 pound of sugar
1 quart of water
Juice of two lemons

Add the sugar and the lemon juice to the raspberries, stir and stand aside one hour. Press through a sieve, add the water, and freeze as directed on page 63.

This will serve eight persons.

## ROMAN PUNCH

Make one quart of lemon water ice. When ready to serve, fill it into small punch glasses, make a little well in the centre and fill the space with good Jamaica rum.

This will serve eight persons.

## SOUR SOP SHERBET OR ICE

Squeeze the juice from one large sour sop, strain, and add four tablespoonfuls of sugar, boiled a moment with four tablespoonfuls of water. Freeze as directed on page 63.

A quart of sour sop when frozen will serve six persons.

## CRANBERRY SHERBET

1 pint of cranberries
½ pound of sugar
½ pint of water

Add the water to the cranberries, cover, bring to a boil; press through a colander, return them to the fire, add the sugar, and stir until the sugar dissolves. Take from the fire, and, when cold, freeze, stirring slowly all the while.

Serve with the meat course at dinner.

This will serve eight persons.

## CUCUMBER SORBET

2 large cucumbers
2 tart apples
1 pint of water
1 teaspoonful of sugar
½ teaspoonful of salt
1 tablespoonful of gelatin
1 saltspoonful of black pepper
Juice of one lemon

Peel the cucumbers, cut them into halves and remove the seeds. Dissolve the gelatin in a half cupful of hot water. Grate the flesh of the cucumbers; grate the apples, add them to the cucumbers, and add all the other ingredients. Freeze as you would ordinary sherbet.

Serve in tiny glasses, with boiled cod or halibut.

This will fill eight small stem glasses.

## GOOSEBERRY SORBET

½ pint of gooseberry jam
4 tablespoonfuls of sugar
1 pint of water
Juice of one lemon

Mix all the ingredients together and freeze, turning slowly all the while. Serve in small glasses.

This is usually served at Christmas dinner with goose.

This will serve six persons.

## ORANGE SHERBET

1 pint of orange juice
2 tablespoonfuls of gelatin
¾ pound of sugar
1 pint of water

Cover the gelatin with an extra half cupful of cold water and soak for a half hour. Add the sugar to the pint of water and stir it over the fire until it boils; add the grated yellow rind of two oranges and the juice; strain through a fine sieve and freeze, turning the freezer slowly all the while. Remove the dasher, stir in a meringue made from the white of one egg, and repack to ripen for an hour at least.

This will serve six persons.

## MINT SHERBET

2 dozen stalks of spearmint
½ pound of sugar
1 quart of water
Juice of three lemons

Strip the leaves from the stalks of the mint, chop them to a pulp and rub them with the sugar. Add the water, bring to a boil, boil five minutes, and, when cold, add three drops of green coloring and the juice of the lemons; strain and freeze, turning slowly all the while.

Serve at dinner with mutton or lamb.

This will serve six persons; in small stem glasses, eight persons.

## TOMATO SORBET OR SHERBET

1 quart can or
12 fresh tomatoes
1 slice of onion
1 blade of mace
1 saltspoonful of celery seed
1 pint of water
1 teaspoonful of salt
1 teaspoonful of paprika
1 tablespoonful of gelatin
Juice of one lemon
A dash of cayenne

Add all the ingredients to the tomatoes, stir over the fire until the mixture reaches the boiling point, boil five minutes, and strain through a fine sieve. When this is cold, freeze according to the rule for sherbets, turning slowly all the time.

Serve in punch glasses at dinner as an accompaniment to roasted beef, or venison, or saddle of mutton.

If fresh tomatoes are used, simply cut them into halves and cook them without peeling.

This will fill nine or ten punch glasses.

# Frozen Fruits

Frozen fruits are mixed and frozen the same as water ices, that is, they are only stirred occasionally while freezing, but the fruit must be mashed or it will form little balls of ice through a partly frozen mixture. The only difference between a water ice and a frozen fruit is that the mixture is not strained, and more fruit and less water is used. If canned fruits are used, and these recipes followed, cut down the sugar. Cream may be used in place of water with sub-acid fruits.

## FROZEN APRICOTS

1 quart of apricots
2 tablespoonfuls of gelatin
1 cupful of sugar
1 pint of cream

Drain the apricots from the can, mash them through a colander, add the sugar and stir until the sugar is dissolved. Cover the gelatin with a half cupful of cold water and soak for a half hour. Stand it over hot water, stir until dissolved, add it to the apricot mixture, and freeze. When frozen, remove the dasher and stir in the cream whipped to a stiff froth. Repack and stand aside two hours to ripen.

This will serve ten persons.

## FROZEN BANANAS

12 large ripe bananas
1 pound of sugar
½ pint of water
1 pint of cream
Juice of two lemons

Peel the bananas and mash them through a colander. Add the sugar to the water, and boil five minutes; when cold, add the lemon juice and the bananas. Put the mixture into a freezing can, stir slowly until frozen. Remove the dasher and stir in carefully the cream whipped to a stiff froth.

This will serve ten or twelve persons.

## FROZEN CHOCOLATE

1 quart of milk
3 ounces of chocolate
2/3 cupful of sugar
1 pint of water
½ pint of cream, whipped
1 teaspoonful of vanilla

Grate the chocolate and put it in a double boiler with the water and sugar; let the water in the surrounding boiler boil fifteen minutes, beat well, and add the milk. Stir until thoroughly mixed, and the milk is very hot. Take from the fire, add the vanilla, and when the mixture is cold, freeze, turning slowly all the while. Serve in chocolate cups with the whipped cream on top.

This will fill nine chocolate cups.

## FROZEN PINEAPPLE

2 large pineapples
1 quart of water
1 pound of sugar
Juice of one lemon

Peel the pineapples and grate them. Add the sugar to the water, stir until the sugar is dissolved, boil five minutes and cool; add the pineapple and lemon juice, and freeze, turning the freezer slowly.

This will serve eight or ten persons.

## FROZEN COFFEE

1 quart of cold water
½ pound of sugar
6 heaping tablespoonfuls of finely ground coffee
½ pint of cream

Put the coffee and the water in a double boiler over the fire, and let the water in the surrounding boiler boil for at least twenty minutes after it begins to boil. Strain through two thicknesses of cheese cloth, add the sugar, stir until the sugar is dissolved, and stand aside until very cold. Add the cream and the unbeaten white of one egg. Freeze, turning the freezer slowly. This should be the consistency of a soft mush and very light.

Serve in coffee cups, either plain or with whipped cream on top.

This will serve six persons.

## FROZEN PEACHES, No. 1

2 pounds of very ripe peaches
6 peach kernels
1 pint of water
½ pound of sugar
Juice of one lemon

Crack the kernels, chop them fine, add them to the sugar, add the water, and boil five minutes; strain and stand aside to cool. Pare the peaches, press them through a colander, add them to the cold syrup, turn into the freezer, and stir slowly until the mixture is frozen. If the peaches are colorless, add a few drops of cochineal before freezing.

This will serve eight persons.

## FROZEN PEACHES, No. 2

1 quart of peach pulp
1 pint of cream
¾ pound of sugar
Juice of one lemon

Add the lemon juice to the peach pulp, add the sugar, and stand aside, stirring every now and then until the sugar is dissolved. Freeze the mixture, stirring slowly; when frozen, remove the dasher, and fold in the cream whipped to a stiff froth.

This is one of the nicest ices for afternoon or evening collations.

This will serve eight persons; in stem glasses, ten persons.

## FROZEN RASPBERRIES

1 quart of raspberries
¾ pound of sugar
1 pint of water
Juice of one lemon

Add the sugar and the lemon juice to the berries, mash them with a potato masher. Let them stand one hour, add the water, and freeze.

This will serve eight persons.

## FROZEN WATERMELON

Scrape the centre from a very ripe watermelon, chop quickly and press through a colander. To each pint of this juice, add a half cupful of sugar and four tablespoonfuls of sherry. Freeze until it is like wet snow. Serve in glasses.

One pint will fill three stem glasses.

### FROZEN STRAWBERRIES

1 quart of very ripe strawberries
1 pound of sugar
1 pint of water
Juice of one lemon

Add the sugar and lemon juice to the berries, let them stand one hour. Mash the berries through a colander, add the water, and freeze, turning the dasher constantly but very slowly.

This will serve eight persons.

# Frappé

A frappé is nothing more nor less than a water ice partly frozen. For instance, Café Frappé is a partly frozen coffee. The mixture looks like wet snow. A Champagne Frappé is champagne packed in salt and ice and the bottles agitated until the champagne is partly frozen.

# Parfait

A parfait is a dessert made from frozen whipped cream, sweetened and flavored. An old fashioned parfait was not frozen in an ice cream freezer; the mixture was packed at once into a mold, the mold packed in salt and ice to freeze for two or three hours. To be perfect, the mixture must be frozen on the outside to the depth of one and a half to two inches, with a soft centre. The quick parfait given under frozen desserts is now in general use.

# Mousse

A mousse is a parfait frozen to the centre. These mixtures are not smooth like ice cream, but are frozen in crystals and to be exactly correct, should look like moss when cut.

### BURNT ALMOND MOUSSE

¼ pound of Jordan almonds
2 ounces of almond paste
2/3 cupful of powdered sugar
1 pint of thick cream
1 teaspoonful of almond extract

Whip the cream to a very stiff froth. Blanch, toast and grind the almonds, putting them through an ordinary meat grinder; rub them with the almond paste, adding the extract and about two tablespoonfuls of water or sherry. Sprinkle the sugar over the whipped cream, and then fold in the nut mixture. Pack at once into a mold, put on the lid, fasten the seam with a strip of muslin dipped in paraffin or melted suet, and pack in coarse salt and ice to freeze for two or three hours.

Serve plain or dusted with chopped almonds. This will serve six persons.

## COFFEE MOUSSE

1 pint of cream
½ cupful of powdered sugar
2 tablespoonfuls of coffee extract

Whip the cream to a stiff froth, sprinkle over the sugar, add the coffee extract, and, when well mixed, pack and freeze.

This will serve six persons.

## EGYPTIAN MOUSSE

½ cupful of rice
1 tablespoonful of gelatin
2/3 cupful of sugar
¼ pound of dates
½ pint of milk
1 pint of cream
1 teaspoonful of vanilla

Wash the rice, throw it into boiling water, boil rapidly twenty minutes; drain, add the milk, and cook in a double boiler fifteen minutes. Add the sugar, the gelatin that has been moistened in cold water, and the dates chopped. Take from the fire, add the vanilla, and when the mixture is cold, fold in carefully the whipped cream. Freeze as directed in a mold, and serve with cold quince jelly sauce.

This will serve ten persons.

## DUCHESS MOUSSE

4 eggs
½ cupful of sugar
1 pint of cream
1 teaspoonful of vanilla
5 drops of cochineal

Beat the yolks of the eggs and the sugar until very, very light; fold in the whites of the eggs and the flavoring. Stand the bowl in a pan of boiling water and beat continuously until the ingredients are hot; take from the fire and beat constantly for ten minutes. When this is cool, fold in the cream whipped to a stiff froth, pack and freeze.

Serve with quince jelly sauce poured over the mousse.

This will serve eight persons.

## PISTACHIO MOUSSE

4 ounces of pistachio nuts
1 tablespoonful of gelatin
1 pint of water
1 pint of cream
½ pound of sugar
1 teaspoonful of almond extract
3 drops of green coloring

Blanch the pistachio nuts and put them through a meat grinder. Boil the sugar and water for five minutes; when cool, add the coloring, the pistachio nuts, and the gelatin moistened in a little cold water. When this is cold, fold in the cream beaten to a stiff froth, and freeze in a mold as directed.

If this is not too well mixed the cream will separate, which makes the handsomer dessert. When the mousse is turned from the mold it will then have a solid white base with a rather green, beautiful transparent mixture at the top.

This will serve ten persons.

## RICE MOUSSE WITH A COMPOTE OF MANDARINS

½ cupful of rice
1 tablespoonful of gelatin
2/3 cupful of sugar
1 pint of milk
1 pint of cream
¼ pound of candied cherries
1 teaspoonful of vanilla

Wash and boil the rice in water for twenty minutes, drain, put it in a double boiler with the milk and sugar; stir until the sugar is dissolved, cover the kettle and cook slowly for twenty minutes. Press through a sieve, add the vanilla, and the gelatin covered with cold water. When this is cold, fold in the cream whipped to a stiff froth; pack and freeze.

I usually freeze this in the ordinary ice cream can; simply remove the dasher, put in the mixture and pack it to freeze for two or three hours.

While this is ripening, separate the mandarins into carpels. Boil together for five minutes one pound of sugar, a half pint of water and the juice of one lemon; take from the fire, add at once the carpels, stir lightly until they are thoroughly covered with the syrup and stand aside until *very cold.*

At serving time, wipe the outside of the freezing can with a warm towel, turn the mousse into the centre of a round dish, heap the carpels around the base and over the top in the form of a pyramid, pour over the syrup, and send at once to the table.

This will serve twelve persons.

# Sauces for Ice Creams

## HOT CHOCOLATE SAUCE

½ cupful of cream or condensed milk
2 ounces of chocolate
1 cupful of sugar
1 teaspoonful of vanilla

Put all the ingredients into a saucepan and stir over the fire until they reach boiling point, boil until the mixture slightly hardens when dropped into cold water. Add the vanilla, turn at once into the sauceboat and send to the table. This must be sufficiently thin to dip nicely over the ice cream.

## MAPLE SAUCE

1 cupful of sugar
1 teaspoonful of lemon juice
1 cupful of water
1 teaspoonful of maple flavoring

Put half the sugar in an iron saucepan and stand it over the fire until it melts and browns, add hastily the water, the remaining sugar and the lemon juice, and boil for about two minutes; take from the fire and add the flavoring. This may be served plain, or with chopped fruit or nuts added.

## CLARET SAUCE

Boil one cupful of sugar and a half cupful of water with a saltspoonful of cream of tartar for five minutes. Take from the fire and add one cupful of claret, and stand aside until icy cold.

## NUT SAUCE

1 cupful of sugar
½ cupful of chopped nuts
1 cupful of water
1 teaspoonful of caramel
2 teaspoonfuls of sherry

Boil the sugar and water with a saltspoonful of cream of tartar or a teaspoonful of lemon juice for five minutes, take from the fire and add all the other ingredients, and stand aside to cool.

## MONTROSE SAUCE

½ tablespoonful of granulated gelatin
¼ cupful of sugar
½ cupful of milk
1 pint of cream
2 tablespoonfuls of brandy
1 teaspoonful of vanilla
Yolks of 3 eggs

Cover the gelatin with milk, let it soak a half hour, and put it, with the milk, in a double boiler over the fire. Beat the yolks of the eggs and the sugar together, add them to the hot milk, stir about one minute until the mixture begins to thicken, take from the fire, and, when cold, add the vanilla and the brandy, and, if you like it, four tablespoonfuls of sherry. Stand this aside until very, very cold.

## ORANGE SAUCE

½ pint of orange juice
½ pint of water
½ cupful of sugar
1 tablespoonful of arrowroot
Whites of three eggs

Add the sugar to the water, and, when boiling hot, add the arrowroot moistened. Beat the whites of the eggs to a stiff froth, add gradually the hot mixture, beating all the while. Add the orange juice, beat again. Turn it into a sauceboat and stand aside until very cold.

## WALNUT SAUCE

Melt maple sugar with a little water, and add to each cupful of syrup a half cupful of chopped black walnuts. Maple syrup may also be used by adding half the quantity of boiling water and the nuts.

# Refreshments for Affairs

# Refreshments for Affairs

In arranging this matter, I have made an earnest effort to be of service to the housewife without or with one maid, as well as to those who are fortunate enough to have trained help.

It is, perhaps, unnecessary to say that elaborate refreshments are entirely out of place at small afternoon or evening cards. An ice, with a wafer, or cake and coffee, served on card tables, are sufficient. A salad, with bread and butter sandwiches and coffee, or a salad sandwich with coffee, make a nice combination. Hot dishes, even light entrées, seem to call for a dessert, or another course and coffee. For wedding and other large receptions serve a greater variety of dishes—jellied meats, boned chicken, salads, sandwiches, ices, cakes and coffee. In winter creamed dishes may be served in paper cases on the same plate with salads and other cold dishes. Serve coffee in small cups after refreshments.

Many so called elaborate dishes are quite easily made, and entrées are frequently quite as good when rewarmed.

Chicken croquettes may be made and fried early in the day, ready to rewarm on brown paper in a baking pan in a hot oven ten minutes before serving time. Sandwiches will keep perfectly well for several hours if wrapped in a damp towel and closed in a tin bread box. Salad sandwiches are better, however, if made as near serving time as possible.

If a large reception is to be given, even with good help, prepare as many dishes as possible the day before, to avoid confusion on the fixed day.

Refreshments for small affairs need not necessarily cost much time or money. A half cupful of chopped left-over steak, a couple of chops or a bit of chicken or a box of sardines, make a good foundation for molds of tomato jelly. Served with bread and butter sandwiches and coffee they are quite sufficient for afternoon or evening cards.

Many of the ices in this book are new and attractive. The new sorbets are liked by those who are always striving for a change. Many are old and reliable.

At large affairs, serve from the dining table.

At card parties, large and small, serve on the card tables, using a small tea cloth on each table.

At afternoon teas, serve from the tea table in the drawing room.

At lawn parties, serve from a large table on the lawn. Small tables may be placed here and there for the convenience of guests.

Every day afternoon tea may be served, in the summer on the porch, in the winter, in the living room or library.

If two dishes only are served, be sure that they harmonize with each other and with the manner of service.

Suitable and hygienic combinations are always to be considered, but the æsthetic side seems to me of equal importance.

## COFFEE FOR LARGE HOME AFFAIRS

Allow eleven ounces of finely ground coffee to each gallon of water. This will serve twenty five persons with one coffee cup each, and forty persons with after-dinner cups. The better way to make a large quantity of coffee without an urn is to purchase a new wash boiler. Wash it and put in the required quantity of water (cold). Weigh the coffee and divide it into half pound lots. Put each lot in a small cheese cloth bag; tie the top of the bag, allowing room for the coffee to swell. Put the bags in the water an hour before serving time, bring slowly to a boil, and then boil rapidly for five minutes. Remove the bags at once, pressing them well. Keep the coffee very hot until it is all served.

Coffee is not spoiled by being kept at boiling point for some time, if the grounds are removed.

# Soups

## BOUILLON

2 pounds of chopped lean beef
2 quarts of cold water
1 small onion
12 cloves
2 tablespoonfuls of sugar
2 teaspoonfuls of salt
12 whole peppercorns
A dash of cayenne
Juice of half a lemon

Put the sugar in the soup kettle, add the onion, sliced, and shake until the onion is thoroughly browned and the sugar almost burned; add the meat, shake it for a moment, and add the water. Cover, bring to boiling point, and put over a slow fire to simmer for two hours. Add all the seasonings and simmer one hour longer. Strain through a colander, pressing the meat. Beat the whites of two eggs slightly, then whisk them into the warm bouillon, and add the juice of the lemon. Bring to boiling point, boil rapidly five minutes, let it stand a moment, and strain through two thicknesses of cheese cloth. This should stand until it is perfectly cold, so that every particle of fat may be removed from the surface. Reheat to serve.

This will serve ten persons, using ordinary bouillon cups.

## CLAM BOUILLON

50 large clams
2 quarts of water
12 whole peppercorns
½ teaspoonful of celery seed

Wash and scrub the clams thoroughly. Put them, a few at a time, in the soup kettle, the bottom of which has been covered with a pint of boiling water. Boil rapidly, take the clams out with a skimmer, and put in another lot, and so continue until all the clams have been cooked. Remove them from the shells, saving all the liquor. Chop and return them, with the liquor and remaining water, to the soup kettle. Simmer gently a half hour, then add the peppercorns, crushed, and the celery seed. Cover the kettle, take it from the fire and allow it to stand until perfectly cold. Strain through two thicknesses of cheese cloth. Reheat to serve.

This will serve fifteen persons.

## BELLEVUE BOUILLON

1 quart of plain or chicken bouillon
1 quart of clam bouillon
½ pint of cream
Paprika

This is one of the most elegant of all bouillons. Heat the bouillons separately, mix them at the last minute, pour at once into heated cups, put a tablespoonful of whipped cream on the top of each cup, garnish with a dusting of paprika, and send to the table.

This will serve ten persons; in a pinch, twelve.

## CHICKEN BOUILLON

1 four pound fowl
3 quarts of water
1 onion
2 tablespoonfuls of sugar
1 teaspoonful of salt
1 bay leaf
1 saltspoonful of celery seed, or one half cupful of chopped celery
1 saltspoonful of black pepper

Draw the chicken and cut it up as for a fricassee. Scald and skin the feet, and crack them thoroughly with your cleaver knife. Put the sugar in a soup kettle, add the onion, sliced, shake over a quick fire until brown, add the chicken and the water, bring to boiling point, and skim. Simmer gently for two hours. Add all the seasonings, simmer one hour longer, and strain. Add the juice of half a lemon and the whites of two eggs, slightly beaten. Boil rapidly five minutes, and strain through two thicknesses of cheese cloth. Reheat to serve. This may be used in place of beef bouillon, with the clam broth, for Bellevue bouillon.

This will serve twelve persons.

## OYSTER BOUILLON

50 fat oysters
2 quarts of water
12 whole peppercorns
12 whole allspice
1½ teaspoonfuls of salt

Drain and wash the oysters. Throw them at once in a hot kettle, shake until the gills have curled, cover the kettle, and simmer gently for fifteen minutes. Drain again, this time saving the liquor. Return it to the kettle with the peppercorns and allspice, crushed, and water. Chop the oysters with a silver knife, put them back in the kettle, simmer gently a half hour, and add the salt. Strain through two thicknesses of cheese cloth, reheat and serve with whipped cream on top of each cup.

This serves fifteen persons.

## TOMATO PUREE à la RORER

1 quart can of tomatoes
½ pint of cream
1 quart of chicken bouillon
2 tablespoonfuls of butter
2 tablespoonfuls of arrowroot
1 bay leaf
1 blade of mace
1 onion
1 teaspoonful of salt
1 teaspoonful of paprika

Add the onion, paprika, mace and bay leaf to the tomatoes, boil rapidly five minutes. Moisten the arrowroot with three or four tablespoonfuls of cold water, add it to the hot tomato, boil ten minutes, and press through a sieve. Add the chicken bouillon, boil ten minutes, add the butter, and, when the butter is thoroughly dissolved, turn at once into cups. Put a tablespoonful of whipped cream on top of each, and serve.

This will serve ten persons.

## GLAZE

Glaze is absolutely necessary for fine cooking, either for the browning of sweetbreads, birds or chickens.

Cover a half box of gelatin with a half cupful of cold water to soak for an hour. Put one quart of good bouillon, chicken or beef, over the fire, and boil it rapidly until reduced to a pint; add the gelatin. As soon as the gelatin is dissolved, strain the mixture. Put four tablespoonfuls of sugar into an iron saucepan, stir until it is browned, then add to it slowly the hot glaze, stir until it is thoroughly melted, turn it into a china or granite receptacle, and stand away to cool. Keep this in the refrigerator, and use it according to directions.

# Sweetbreads

## SWEETBREADS à la CREME, No. 1

2 pairs of calves' sweetbreads
1 can of mushrooms
1 pint of milk
4 level tablespoonfuls of butter
4 level tablespoonfuls of flour
1 level teaspoonful of salt
1 saltspoonful of white pepper

Wash the sweetbreads and trim them. Throw them in a saucepan of boiling water and simmer gently for one hour; drain and throw them in cold water. The water in which they were boiled may be used for stock. When they are thoroughly cold, remove the membrane, and pick them into small pieces. Rub the butter and flour together in a saucepan, add the milk, stir until boiling, add the mushrooms, chopped fine, the sweetbreads, salt and pepper. Stir until it again reaches the boiling point, cover and stand over hot water for twenty minutes. Serve in ramekin dishes, paté shells or paper cases. This will fill twelve cases, or fourteen paté shells.

## SWEETBREADS à la CREME, No. 2

1 pound of fresh mushrooms
2 pairs of calves' sweetbreads
½ pint of milk
4 level tablespoonfuls of butter
4 level tablespoonfuls of flour
1 teaspoonful of salt
1 saltspoonful of white pepper

Wash and stem the mushrooms; do not peel them. With a silver knife cut them into slices. Put half the butter in a saucepan, add the mushrooms and half the milk, and the salt and pepper. Cover the saucepan, and stew slowly a half hour. Rub the remaining butter and flour together; drain the liquor from the mushrooms, add it, with the rest of the milk, to the butter and flour. Stir until boiling, add the mushrooms and sweetbreads that have been boiled and picked apart. Cover the saucepan, stand it over hot water, or use a double boiler, pushing the boiler to the back of the stove for twenty to thirty minutes. The saucepan must be kept closely covered, or the aroma of the mushrooms will be lost.

This will fill sixteen cases, or fourteen paté shells, or alone it will serve twelve persons.

## SWEETBREADS à la BORDELAISE

1 pair of calves' sweetbreads
½ pint of stock
1 onion
1 bay leaf
½ teaspoonful of salt
1 can of mushrooms
1 teaspoonful of browning or kitchen bouquet
1 saltspoonful of white pepper
2 level tablespoonfuls of butter
2 level tablespoonfuls of flour

Wash the sweetbreads, put them in a saucepan, add the bay leaf, onion and one pint of cold water; bring to boiling point, and simmer gently one hour. Save the water in which they were boiled. Throw the sweetbreads into cold water, remove the membrane and pick them apart. Put the butter and flour in a saucepan; when thoroughly mixed, add a half pint of stock in which the sweetbreads were boiled, stir until boiling, add the mushrooms, drained, and the seasoning. Bring to boiling point, and push to the back of the fire for ten minutes. Skim off any butter that comes to the surface, add the sweetbreads, cook gently ten minutes longer, and serve in either paté cases, ramekin dishes, or paper cases.

This will serve eight persons.

## BAKED SWEETBREADS

2 pairs of calves' sweetbreads
1 can of French peas
3 tablespoonfuls of butter
2 tablespoonfuls of glaze
1 teaspoonful of salt
1 saltspoonful of pepper

Wash the sweetbreads and soak them in cold water; cut them apart and trim them neatly. Sprinkle the bottom of a baking pan with a chopped onion, put the sweetbreads on top, dust them lightly with salt and pepper, baste them with one tablespoonful of the butter, melted, and run them in a quick oven to bake for twenty minutes. Then brush them thoroughly with glaze and bake them ten minutes longer. Drain, wash and heat the peas, add the remaining butter and season them with salt and pepper. Put the peas in the bottom of the serving dish, dish the sweetbreads in them and send at once to the table. These may also be served in individual dishes, cutting the sweetbreads in small pieces, so they may be eaten with a fork.

They will serve from four to six people. The throat sweetbread may be cut into halves, but as a rule one sweetbread is served to each person.

## LAMBS' SWEETBREADS IN PAPER CASES

8 lambs' sweetbreads
½ box of gelatin
1 pint of beef stock or chicken bouillon
1 can of peas
1 head of celery
2 level tablespoonfuls of butter
2 level tablespoonfuls of flour
½ pint of milk
1 lemon
Hearts of lettuce
Yolks of two eggs
Salt and pepper

Wash the sweetbreads, put them in a saucepan, cover with boiling water, add two tablespoonfuls of vinegar and a sliced onion. Cook gently for three-quarters of an hour. Drain, put them in a baking pan, brush them with butter, add a few tablespoonfuls of glaze or stock, put over three or four slices of bacon, and cook in the oven a half hour, basting three or four times. Rub the butter and flour together, add the milk, stir until boiling, add two tablespoonfuls of the soaked gelatin, a half teaspoonful of salt and a little white pepper. Take from the fire and add hastily the beaten yolks of the eggs. Cover the bottom of a cold baking pan with muffin rings, put one sweetbread into each muffin ring. When the sauce is a little cool, cover the sweetbreads thoroughly, filling the rings quite full. Stand these away over night in a cold place.

Dissolve the remaining gelatin in the hot bouillon, season, add the lemon juice, and stand it aside over night. At serving time, remove the contents from the rings and place them in paper cases of the same size. Turn the clear aspic out on to a towel and cut it into pretty shapes. Decorate the top of the cases with this aspic, placing a sprig of green in the centre. Drain and press the cold peas through a sieve, and season them with salt and pepper; put this pulp in a pastry bag with a star tube, and decorate the top of each mold. Serve at once with mayonnaise passed in a boat.

Another way is to fill the bottom of the paper cases with finely chopped celery, mixed with mayonnaise, and put the sweetbreads on top, omitting the peas. If made well, these are exceedingly handsome. One "ring" will be served to each person.

## SWEETBREADS à la NEWBURG

2 pairs of calves' sweetbreads
1 can of mushrooms
4 hard boiled yolks of eggs
½ pint of milk
2 level tablespoonfuls of butter
1 tablespoonful of flour
½ teaspoonful of salt
1 saltspoonful of white pepper
½ saltspoonful of grated nutmeg
A dash of cayenne

Cook the sweetbreads as directed in first recipe; when cold, pick them apart, rejecting the membrane. Rub the butter and flour together, add the milk, stir until boiling, and add this slowly to the mashed yolks of the eggs. Work and stir until you have a perfectly smooth paste. Press it through a fine sieve, add the salt, pepper, mushrooms and sweetbreads. Stand over hot water for twenty minutes, until thoroughly hot. Add, if you use it, four tablespoonfuls of sherry, and serve.

This will serve ten persons.

# Shell-Fish Dishes

## DEVILED CRABS

12 crabs, or one pint of crab flake
4 hard boiled eggs
2 level tablespoonfuls of butter
2 tablespoonfuls of soft bread crumbs
1 tablespoonful of flour
1 teaspoonful of salt
1 saltspoonful of grated nutmeg
1 teaspoonful of onion juice
½ pint of milk
A dash of cayenne

Chop the whites of the hard boiled eggs very, very fine. Put the yolks through a sieve. Rub the butter and flour together, and add the milk; stir until boiling, take from the fire, and add the bread crumbs and the eggs. Add all the seasoning to the crab flake, mix the two together, and fill at once into the shells. The shells must be quite full, so that there will be no danger of the fat being held in the shell. Dip the shells in egg, then cover them thickly with bread crumbs. It is well to egg and bread crumb the upper side again; in fact both dippings may be on the upper sides, leaving the shells red underneath. Put these in a frying basket and fry for a minute in hot, deep fat. Serve one to each person.

This quantity should fill eight shells.

## CRAB BACKS à la CARACAS

1 dozen crabs, or six backs and a pint of crab flake
1 teaspoonful of salt
1 teaspoonful of onion juice
A dash of cayenne

Add the seasoning to the crab flakes, and mix without breaking the flakes. Fill the mixture into the backs, put a teaspoonful of butter on the top of each, sprinkle lightly with crumbs, and bake in a quick oven twenty minutes.

## CRAB MEAT à la DEWEY

1 pint of crab flake
2 tablespoonfuls of butter
2 tablespoonfuls of flour
1 teaspoonful of salt
1 red and one green pepper
½ pint of chicken stock, or milk
2 tablespoonfuls of sherry
Yolks of two eggs

Drop the peppers into hot fat just a moment and rub off the skin, remove the seeds and chop the flesh fine. Put this, with the butter, in a saucepan, and shake over the fire until the peppers are soft. Add the flour, mix, and add the stock or milk; stir until boiling, add the salt and pepper and the crab flakes. Do not stir, but heat slowly over hot water. When hot, add the yolks of the eggs, beaten with two tablespoonfuls of cream. Heat again, just a moment, being careful not to curdle the eggs, and serve on toast.

This dish is very nice when made in a chafing dish, and will serve six people.

## LOBSTER CUTLETS

1 pint of lobster meat
2 level tablespoonfuls of butter
4 level tablespoonfuls of flour
½ pint of milk
1 teaspoonful of salt
1 teaspoonful of onion juice
1 saltspoonful of white pepper
½ saltspoonful of grated nutmeg
Yolk of one egg
A dash of cayenne

Chop the boiled lobster rather fine with a silver knife, and add to it all the seasoning. Rub the butter and flour together in a saucepan, add the milk, stir until you have a smooth, thick paste, add the yolk of the egg, cook a moment longer, add the lobster, and turn out to cool. When cold, form into cutlet shaped croquettes, dip in egg, roll in bread crumbs, and fry in deep hot fat. Put a small claw in the end of each cutlet to represent the bone. Serve with these either cream sauce or sauce tartar.

This quantity should make eight cutlets.

## LOBSTER NEWBURG

Make this precisely the same as crabs Newburg, using one pint of boiled lobster meat. Cut the lobster in cubes of about one inch. Purchase one large or two small lobsters.

## OYSTER CROQUETTES

50 fat oysters
4 level tablespoonfuls of flour
2 level tablespoonfuls of butter
1 tablespoonful of chopped parsley
1 teaspoonful of salt
1 teaspoonful of onion juice
½ saltspoonful of nutmeg
1 saltspoonful of white pepper
Yolks of two eggs

Drain and wash the oysters, throw them into a hot kettle, shake until the gills curl and the liquid boils. Boil five minutes and drain, saving the liquor. There should be a half cupful of liquor. Chop the oysters and add them to the liquor. Rub the butter and flour together, add the oysters and liquor, stir until the mixture reaches boiling point, and push to the back of the stove where it will cook for ten minutes. Add all the seasoning and the yolks of the eggs, cook just a minute, and turn out to cool. This must stand either over night, or must be placed directly on the ice for at least four hours. When cold, form into small cylinder shaped croquettes, dip in egg and bread crumbs, and fry in deep hot fat.

This quantity will make one dozen good sized cylinders.

# Poultry and Game Dishes

## CHICKEN CROQUETTES

1 four pound chicken
½ pint of milk
2 level tablespoonfuls of butter
4 level tablespoonfuls of flour
2 teaspoonfuls of salt
2 teaspoonfuls of onion juice
2 tablespoonfuls of chopped parsley
1 saltspoonful of grated nutmeg
1 saltspoonful of white pepper
A dash of cayenne

Draw, truss the chicken, put it into boiling water, boil it rapidly for ten minutes, and let it simmer until tender. When cold, remove the meat, rejecting the bones and skin. Chop the meat with a chopping knife; do not put it through the meat grinder. When fine, add all the seasoning and mix thoroughly. Put the milk in a saucepan over the fire, and add the butter and flour, rubbed together. Stir and cook until you have a smooth paste, add the chicken, mix thoroughly, and turn out to cool. When cold, form into croquettes, dip in an egg, beaten with a tablespoonful of water, roll in dry bread crumbs, and fry in deep hot fat. Serve plain, or with French peas.

This will make thirteen large croquettes.

One pair of thoroughly cooked sweetbreads may be chopped with the chicken, or you may add a pair of parboiled calf's brains; this increases quantity, and makes the croquettes more creamy.

This should make sixteen large cylinders or pyramids, serving sixteen persons.

The meat from the chicken after it is chopped should measure one quart. Any other meat may be substituted for chicken, but could not be used, of course, for an elegant affair.

## CHICKEN à la CREME

The white meat of one cooked chicken
1 pair of calves' sweetbreads
1 can of mushrooms
4 level tablespoonfuls of butter
4 level tablespoonfuls of flour
1 pint of milk
1 teaspoonful of salt
1 saltspoonful of white pepper
10 drops of onion juice
Yolks of two eggs

Cut the chicken into cubes of a half inch. Boil the sweetbreads and pick them apart, rejecting the membrane. Drain and wash the mushrooms, cut them into halves and mix them with the sweetbread and chicken. Rub the butter and flour together, and add the milk; when boiling, add salt, pepper, onion juice and meat. Stand this over hot water in a covered saucepan for twenty minutes, add the yolks of the eggs, slightly beaten, and bring just to boiling point.

Served in ramekins or paper cases this is sufficient for fifteen persons. Served as a supper or luncheon dish alone, twelve persons.

## CHICKEN à la KING

The white meat of one chicken
½ can of mushrooms
1 green pepper
½ pint of milk
½ teaspoonful of salt
2 level tablespoonfuls of butter
2 level tablespoonfuls of flour
1 saltspoonful of white pepper
2 tablespoonfuls of sherry

Drop the pepper into hot fat for a moment to remove the skin, then chop it very fine. Put the butter in a saucepan or chafing dish, add the pepper, stir until the pepper is soft, add the flour, mix and add the milk, stir until boiling, and add the salt. Cut the meat into pieces an inch square, add them to the hot sauce, add the mushrooms, sliced, and, when hot, add the wine and serve.

This will serve four or five persons.

## BOUDINS à la REINE

1 pint of chopped cooked chicken
½ can of mushrooms
1 can of peas
2 eggs
½ cupful of bread crumbs
½ cupful of chicken stock
1 teaspoonful of salt
1 saltspoonful of pepper

Brush ordinary timbale cups lightly with butter, put a mushroom in the centre of the bottom, and around the edge a ring of peas. Put the stock and bread over the fire, and, when boiling, add the chicken and seasonings, stir until it reaches the boiling point, take from the fire, and add the eggs, well beaten. Put this carefully in the cups, cover the top with oiled paper, stand the cups in a shallow pan partly filled with hot water, and cook in the oven about twenty minutes, until the contents are "set" in the centre. Heat the remaining quantity of peas, and season them with salt and pepper. Turn the boudins on a platter, surround them with the hot peas, and send them at once to the table.

This will serve eight persons.

These may also be served with plain sauce, or with Sauce Bechamel.

## SAUCE BECHAMEL

2 level tablespoonfuls of butter
2 level tablespoonfuls of flour
½ cupful of chicken stock
½ cupful of milk
½ teaspoonful of salt
1 saltspoonful of pepper
Yolk of one egg

Rub the butter and flour together, add the liquids, stir until boiling, add the salt and pepper, stir, add the yolk of an egg, well beaten, pass through a fine sieve, and use at once.

## CHICKEN TIMBALE

The white meat of one chicken
½ pint of soft white bread crumbs
½ cupful of milk
1 teaspoonful of salt
1 saltspoonful of white pepper
The whites of five eggs

Put the raw meat of the chicken twice through the meat chopper, then put it in a mortar and pound it to a paste, or work it in a bowl with a wooden spoon. Boil the bread and milk, stirring constantly; when this is cold, add the salt, pepper and four tablespoonfuls of cream; work it gradually into the chicken meat. This must be a perfectly smooth paste. Add the unbeaten whites of two eggs; when they are thoroughly incorporated, fold in the well beaten whites of the three eggs. Put at once into an oiled Charlotte mold or into small timbale molds.

The molds may be garnished with mushrooms, or chopped truffles, or peas. Stand them in a pan of hot water, cover with oiled paper and cook in the oven, small molds twenty-five minutes, a large mold thirty-five. Serve hot, with cream mushroom sauce.

This quantity in small molds should serve twelve people; in a large mold, ten.

## CREAM MUSHROOM SAUCE

1 can of mushrooms
2 level tablespoonfuls of butter
½ pint of milk
2 level tablespoonfuls of flour
½ teaspoonful of salt
1 saltspoonful of pepper

Rub the butter and flour together, and add the milk, stir until boiling, add the seasoning, and the mushrooms, cut into halves. When hot it is ready to use.

# Cold Dishes

## POULET EN BELLEVUE

½ box of gelatin
1 pint of chicken stock
1 bay leaf
1 onion
The white meat of two chickens
Salt and pepper

Remove the white meat carefully from two boiled chickens; split the breasts into halves, long ways. Cover the gelatin with a half cupful of cold water to soak for a half hour. Add the seasonings to the stock or bouillon, bring to a boil, add the gelatin, and if not clear, clarify with the white of an egg. Add the juice of a lemon and strain. Take small oblong china or tin molds, garnish the bottoms with fancy bits of good red pepper and chopped truffles, baste over a little of the hot aspic, and let them stand until very cold. Cool the remaining aspic, but do not allow it to become solid. Put on top of each mold a half breast of chicken, dust with salt and pepper, pour over the cold aspic and stand them aside over night. At serving time dip the molds quickly into hot water, turn out the cutlets, dish them on luncheon plates, and garnish with hearts of lettuce. Pass mayonnaise dressing.

This will make eight molds and serve eight persons. Use the dark meat for fricassee or stew of chicken.

## TOMATOES à l'ALGERIENNE

The white meat of one chicken
24 perfect tomatoes
¼ box of gelatin
½ pint of chicken stock
½ pint of cream
1 teaspoonful of anchovy paste
3 heads of fine lettuce
½ pint of mayonnaise

Peel the tomatoes, cut off the stem end and scoop out the hard portion and the seeds; put the tomatoes on the ice. Put the meat of the chicken through the meat grinder, season it with the anchovy paste, if you have it, and salt and pepper. Soak the gelatin in a half cupful of cold water, add the chicken stock, bring to a boil, add a half teaspoonful of salt, a dash of pepper, and the juice of half a lemon. Mix a part of this with the chicken. Whip the cream, stir it into the chicken mixture, and fill it into the tomatoes, making them smooth on top. When the tomatoes are very cold and the aspic is cool, but not thick, baste just a little over the top, dust thickly with chopped parsley and finely chopped almonds, and stand them in a cold place for several hours. Arrange each tomato in a little nest of lettuce leaves, and pass with them mayonnaise dressing. If these are made well, they are the most sightly of the small cold dishes, and cost almost nothing.

This, of course, will be served to twenty-four persons.

Tongue, sardines, lobster, crab meat or cold left-over meat may be substituted for chicken.

## GALANTINE OF CHICKEN

2 chickens
½ pound of boiled ham
¼ pound of larding pork
1 can of mushrooms
2 teaspoonfuls of salt
1 egg
1 pound of lean veal
2 truffles
Salt and pepper

Singe the chickens, and remove the head and feet; place the chicken on the table with the breast down. Take a small, sharp-pointed sabatier knife and cut the skin from neck to rump right down the back bone. Carefully and slowly run the knife between the bones and the flesh, keeping it always close to the bone. Take out first the wings, then loosen the carcass, and then take out the legs. Unjoint and separate each bone, and take it out as you come to it. Do not take the small bones from the wings; they may be cut off.

When you have removed all the flesh from the bones, keeping it perfectly whole, and without breaking the skin, wipe the skin and put it on the table; draw the legs and the wings inside. Take all the raw meat from the other chicken, rejecting the skin and bones, but you do not have to bone this one carefully. Put it in the meat grinder, with half the ham, all the veal and half the bacon. When chopped, season it with two teaspoonfuls of salt, and two saltspoonfuls of white pepper; add the egg and mix thoroughly. Put a thin layer of this into the boned chicken, put in here and there long pieces of the remaining ham and bacon, a layer of mushrooms, blocks of truffles, then another layer of the forcemeat, and so continue until you have used all the ingredients. Pull up the skin and sew it down the back, making a perfect roll. Tie the neck and rump. Roll this in cheese cloth, fasten it securely, and sew the cheese cloth so that the roll will be perfect when done.

Put all the bones in the soup kettle, add a sliced onion, a bay leaf, and sufficient cold water to come just to the top of the bones. Bring to boiling point, and put in the "galantine," as the chicken roll is called. Cover the kettle, and boil continuously for four hours. When done, slightly cool, remove the cloth, and stand it away until perfectly cold. Strain the water, which should measure two quarts; add to it a box of gelatin that has been soaked in a cupful of water for an hour. Bring this to boiling point, season it with salt and pepper, add the juice of a lemon and the whites of two eggs, slightly beaten. Boil five minutes, and strain through two thicknesses of cheese cloth. Select a long round pudding mold, or a regular boned chicken mold, something like a large melon mold; baste the mold inside with this liquid jelly, decorate it in patterns or unconventional designs, using green and red pepper, the hard boiled white of egg and peas. Allow the remaining jelly to cool, but not stiffen. After you finish the decorations, baste them carefully with cold gelatin and stand the mold on ice. Then put in a little more cold jelly, until you have a good base upon which to rest the "galantine." Put it in, breast side down, and pour over the remaining gelatin. Stand in a cold place for twenty-four hours. When ready to serve, wipe the mold with a warm cloth, and turn the "galantine" on to a long platter. Garnish the platter with hearts of lettuce. To serve, cut the "galantine" in the thinnest possible slices, and serve it with a salad, either celery, or mixed vegetables, or plain lettuce; or it may be served with a sauce tartar or plain mayonnaise dressing.

This is one of the most elegant of cold dishes, and will serve twenty-five persons.

## CHICKEN MOUSSE

1 pint of cooked chopped chicken
½ pint of milk
2 level tablespoonfuls of butter
1 teaspoonful of salt
1 level tablespoonful of flour
1 tablespoonful of granulated gelatin
1 saltspoonful of white pepper
½ pint of cream

Rub the butter and the flour together over the fire, add the milk, stir until boiling, and add the gelatin that has been soaked in a couple of tablespoonfuls of cold water for fifteen minutes. Add the salt, pepper and chicken, mix thoroughly and stand it aside to cool. Beat the cream to a stiff froth. Make a half cupful of mayonnaise from the yolk of one egg and eight tablespoonfuls of olive oil; stir the cream gradually into the mayonnaise and then add it carefully to the cold chicken mixture. Turn it into an ordinary melon pudding mold, cover closely and stand it in a bucket of cracked ice and salt. It is wise to bind the cover seam to keep out the salt water. When slightly frozen, which will take about two hours, remove the lid, turn out the mousse, cover the top with first a ring of hard boiled whites, chopped fine, then a ring of finely chopped parsley, inside this a ring of the yolks of the eggs pressed through a sieve, and right in the centre a sprig of curly parsley. Send at once to the table.

Lobster, crab flakes and cold roasted game may be used according to this recipe.

This will serve eight persons at a reception. At a luncheon only six persons.

## PATE-DE-FOIE-GRAS IN ASPIC

1 box of granulated gelatin
1 teaspoonful of beef extract
1 small onion
1 bay leaf
1 blade of mace
1 truffle
1 carrot
1 green pepper
1 red pepper
1 lemon
1 tureen of foie-gras

Cover the gelatin with a half cupful of cold water to soak for a half hour. Put all the vegetables and seasoning in one quart of cold water, bring to boiling point, simmer gently twenty minutes, add the beef extract, one teaspoonful of salt and a saltspoonful of black pepper. Add the gelatin, stir until the gelatin is dissolved, and strain. Add the juice of the lemon and the whites of two eggs, slightly beaten. Bring to boiling point, boil rapidly for five minutes, and strain through two thicknesses of cheese cloth. Cut the peppers into fancy shapes. Chop the truffle fine. Select a dozen dariole molds, moisten them in cold water, baste them with the aspic, and, when cold, garnish the bottoms handsomely with a pepper and truffle. Put in another layer of aspic, which must be cold, but not thick; on top of this place a slice of pate-de-foie-gras, cover them carefully with the aspic, filling the mold to the top. Stand these away over night. Serve on crisp lettuce leaves, and pass with them a mayonnaise. These are the handsomest of all the cold aspic dishes.

A single large mold may be used for ball suppers or large receptions. To serve, cut it into slices, and pass mayonnaise of celery.

This will serve twelve persons.

## BONED TURKEY

Turkey is boned precisely the same as you bone a "galantine" of chicken. Use for the stuffing:

2 chickens
1 pound of sausage meat
1 pound of veal
3 truffles
1 can of mushrooms
1 pound of ham

Take six hours to cook the turkey. When cold put it in a boned turkey mold that has been garnished, and fill with aspic.

Cut in very thin slices to serve thirty persons.

## BONED QUAIL

Purchase twenty-four quails. Split them down the back and remove the bones, keeping your knife close to the bone. Do not break the skin nor tear the flesh. Spread them out, skin side down, on a board and stuff them with the seasoned sausage meat. Put them into shape, sew them down the back, cover the breast of each with a slice of bacon, put them in a baking pan, add a half pint of hot stock, and bake in a quick oven forty minutes, dusting with pepper and basting frequently. When cold, remove the string from the back.

For a dozen quails use:

1 box of gelatin
1 quart of milk
1 tablespoonful of grated onion
2 truffles
4 level tablespoonfuls of butter
4 level tablespoonfuls of flour
2 teaspoonfuls of salt
1 saltspoonful of white pepper

Soak the gelatin in the milk a half hour. Rub the butter and flour together, then add the milk and gelatin, stir until boiling, and add all the seasoning and strain. Stand aside until cool, but not thick. Place the birds on a tin sheet or a large platter, and baste them with this cold white sauce. As soon as the first basting has hardened, baste them again. This time decorate the breasts with the truffles cut into fancy shapes. To serve, arrange them around a large mound of mayonnaise of celery. Use either a meat platter, or two round chop dishes. Have the breasts of the birds down, and the back slightly pressed into the salad. In between each bird put a pretty bunch of curly parsley, and garnish the top of the mound with Spanish peppers cut into strips. Serve one to each person.

# Salads

Salads play a most important part in all conventional suppers Chicken, lobster, crab, duck, tongue, and lamb salad take the place of other meats, although for a large supper there is no objection to serving a meat salad following a hot course. If one can make a good mayonnaise dressing, salads are the easiest of all refreshments, and are most acceptable to the guests.

## MAYONNAISE

Put the yolks of three eggs in a clean cold dish, beat slightly and add slowly, almost drop by drop, a half pint or more of salad oil. After adding the first half pint, add a half teaspoonful of vinegar now and then to prevent breaking. You may add a quart of oil, if you like; you may serve it plain, or stir in at the last moment stiffly whipped cream. One quart of mayonnaise will hold one quart of whipped cream. For light colored salads, as sweetbread and Waldorf, it is well to use the whipped cream slightly colored with a drop of vegetable green.

## SAUCE TARTAR

Add to a half pint of mayonnaise dressing a tablespoonful of chopped gherkin, the same of chopped parsley, four chopped olives and a tablespoonful of capers.

## SAUCE SUEDOISE

½ pint of mayonnaise
½ pint of cream
2 tablespoonfuls of finely grated horseradish

Whip the cream and drain it, then stir it carefully into the mayonnaise, and at last add the horseradish. This sauce is appropriate to serve with boned partridges or quail, and is also nice to serve with mixed cold meats.

## FRENCH DRESSING

Put eight tablespoonfuls of oil in a bowl, add a half teaspoonful of salt, and a piece of ice the size of an egg. Work the ice with the oil until the salt is thoroughly dissolved, then add a tablespoonful of tarragon vinegar and a drop of Tabasco sauce. Remove the ice, beat rapidly until you have a creamy dressing, and use at once. French dressing should be used over cucumber or tomato molds, and is nice with fish or chicken mousse and East Indian Salad.

## CUCUMBER MOLDS

2 good sized cucumbers
½ box of gelatin
1 pint of chicken stock
1 teaspoonful of salt
1 tablespoonful of onion juice
1 saltspoonful of pepper
The juice of one lemon

Peel and grate the cucumbers. Add the gelatin to the stock, soak for twenty minutes, bring to a boil and add the seasoning; then stir in the drained cucumber. Turn into small round timbale cups and stand aside to harden. Serve with any cold fish dish, as cold boiled slice of halibut, or fish in aspic. These are nice for Sunday night supper with broiled sardines.

## TOMATO MOLDS

1 can of tomatoes
1 box of gelatin
1 onion
1 saltspoonful of celery seed
1 bay leaf
1 blade of mace
2 tablespoonfuls of tarragon vinegar
1 teaspoonful of paprika
2 teaspoonfuls of salt

Cover the gelatin with a cupful of cold water to soak for fifteen minutes. Add all the seasoning to the tomatoes, bring to boiling point, add the gelatin, and strain. Turn into twelve small tomato molds and stand aside to harden. Serve with mayonnaise dressing as an accompaniment to boned chicken or turkey, or chicken paté, or alone, with mayonnaise, as a complete salad. Chopped celery, a little cold cooked meat or nuts may be added, when the molds are to be served as a salad. With this addition, one half the recipe will serve twelve persons.

## CRABS RAVIGOT

Purchase as many crab shells as you have people to serve. To each six allow a pint of crab flakes. If you buy the crabs fresh, twelve crabs will serve six people. Squeeze over the flakes the juice of one lemon, add a half teaspoonful of salt and a dash of Tabasco. Fill the meat loosely into the shells, place each shell on a pretty paper doily on a plate, and spread over a thick layer of mayonnaise dressing, with which you have mixed a tablespoonful of chopped parsley, a tablespoonful of tarragon leaves, a tablespoonful of chopped onion or shallot, and a tablespoonful of green chives.

## CHICKEN SALAD

Cut cold boiled chicken into dice, add an equal quantity of tender celery, season with salt, pepper and lemon juice, mix with mayonnaise dressing, and serve on lettuce leaves.

A four pound chicken, and six heads of tender celery, three heads of lettuce, a half pint of whipped cream, and one pint of mayonnaise, will serve fifteen persons.

## LOBSTER SALAD

Cut cold boiled lobster into cubes of an inch, mix with mayonnaise dressing and serve on lettuce leaves.

One three-pound lobster will serve six persons.

## CRAB SALAD

Season crab flakes with salt, pepper and lemon juice, mix them with mayonnaise dressing, and serve on lettuce leaves, garnished with cress.

One pint of flakes will serve six persons.

## TONGUE SALAD

Cut fresh-cooked beef's tongue or calf's tongue into dice. Have ready peeled perfectly round smooth tomatoes, take out the core and scoop out the seeds. Fill each tomato with the cubes of tongue, sprinkle over a teaspoonful of lemon juice and a little salt and pepper. Stand these on nests of lettuce leaves, put on top of each a large tablespoonful of mayonnaise. Dust thickly with paprika and serve one to each person.

## LAMB SALAD

Cut cold boiled lamb into dice, mix with it half the quantity of freshly cooked green peas or canned peas. Add a half can of mushrooms, chopped fine, salt, pepper and lemon juice. Mix with mayonnaise dressing and serve on lettuce leaves, garnished with large sprigs of mint. Cap the top of the dish with a good sized sprig of fresh mint, and sprinkle capers all over the salad.

A nice plain lamb salad is made by mixing left-over cold lamb with mayonnaise; serve on lettuce leaves and garnish with chopped mint.

A quart will serve ten persons.

## TOMATOES EN SURPRISE

This is one of the nicest of the salads for a simple card party. It takes the place of both vegetables and meat, and with brown bread and nut sandwiches as an accompaniment, is very attractive. Peel the tomatoes, cut off the stem end and scoop out the core and seeds. Fill the tomatoes with either crab flakes, chopped lobster, canned salmon, or sardines. Squeeze over a little lemon juice, and dust with salt and pepper. Turn them upside down on a nest of lettuce leaves, and cover the tomato with creamy mayonnaise.

## SWEETBREAD SALAD

2 pairs of sweetbreads
4 ounces of almonds
4 ounces of pecan meats
2 ounces of shelled Brazilian nuts
2 Spanish peppers
½ can of mushrooms
2 heads of celery
2 heads of lettuce
1 pint of mayonnaise
1 pint of cream
1 can of French peas

This is the most elaborate of all salads, is palatable and comparatively wholesome. Put the sweetbreads into boiling water, add a tablespoonful of vinegar, and simmer gently for one hour. When cold, remove the membrane and pick the sweetbreads apart. Put them in a bowl, cover them with an onion, sliced, and squeeze over the juice of a lemon; cover the bowl and stand it aside over night. Blanch and chop the almonds, and chop the pecans. Remove the onion from the sweetbreads, mix in the nuts, add the white portions of the celery, cut the size of the sweetbreads. Add the mushrooms, sliced, two teaspoonfuls of salt, a saltspoonful of white pepper and a saltspoonful of paprika. Add the cream, whipped, to the mayonnaise, and mix a portion of it with the sweetbreads and celery. Have a round shallow salad bowl lined with the lettuce leaves, turn in the centre the sweetbread salad and cover it over with the remaining quantity of mayonnaise. Put the peas in a ring around the base of the salad, and cap the top with the yolk of a hard-boiled egg. Cut the white of the egg into eighths and press them upside down around the yolk, forming a sort of a daisy. Cut the Spanish peppers into rings and arrange them just above the peas. Put here and there around the base, above the peas, ripe or green olives, and send to the table.

This will serve at supper or luncheon ten persons.

## ROAST BEEF SALAD

For impromptu evening affairs any cold left-over meat may be utilized in a salad. Beef, mutton and tongue are usually served with French dressing, seasoned with tomato catsup. Cut the meat into dice, season with salt and pepper, dish them on lettuce, or they may be mixed in the winter with chopped celery or chopped crisp cabbage, and basted with French dressing, seasoned with two or three tablespoonfuls of tomato catsup for beef, mint sauce, or a drop of Tabasco Sauce for mutton, a little Worcestershire Sauce for tongue.

A quart will serve ten persons.

## EAST INDIAN SALAD

This is purely a vegetable salad; it is exceedingly nice for a simple evening affair. Shave sufficient cabbage to make a pint, soak it in cold water for one hour, changing the water once or twice. Cover a half box of gelatin with a half cupful of cold water to soak for a half hour. Put a half can of tomatoes in a saucepan, add one onion, chopped, a teaspoonful of salt, a saltspoonful of pepper and the juice of a lemon, or two tablespoonfuls of vinegar. Bring to boiling point, and add the gelatin. Cover the bottom of a large melon mold with finely chopped celery or cooked carrots, put on top of this a few drops of onion juice, then a thin layer of cabbage, a dusting of salt and pepper, then a goodly quantity of India relish; cover this over with chopped nuts, pecans, hickory or peanuts, then another layer of celery, and so continue until the mold is full, seasoning the layers with salt and pepper. Have the last layer chopped celery. Strain over this the tomato aspic, which should be cold, but not thick, and stand aside for four or five hours. Serve plain, or garnished with lettuce leaves or cress.

This will serve twelve persons.

## POTATO SALAD

Fancy potato salad may be served for an evening affair with an accompaniment of cold tongue, or it may be garnished with hard-boiled eggs and form the entire course. Serve with it brown bread and butter and coffee.

- 4 potatoes
- 8 tablespoonfuls of olive oil
- 2 tablespoonfuls of cream
- 2 tablespoonfuls of tarragon vinegar
- 1 level teaspoonful of salt
- 1 saltspoonful of pepper

Wash the potatoes and boil them with skins on. The moment they are done, drain the water, dry and peel. Put the oil, salt, pepper and vinegar in a bowl, beat rapidly until thoroughly mixed, and then add one good sized onion, sliced very thin, or use two tablespoonfuls of grated onion. Put in the hot potatoes, sliced, toss them a moment, and if you have it, sprinkle over two tablespoonfuls of vinegar from pickled walnuts, or a tablespoonful of mushroom catsup. Stand aside to cool. When ready to serve, turn on to a cold platter, garnish with chopped parsley, and, if you have them, chopped pickled beets.

This is sufficient for six persons.

## FRENCH POTATO SALAD

Moisten a teaspoonful of cornstarch in four tablespoonfuls of milk, add two tablespoonfuls of cream and stir over hot water until thick; then add gradually six tablespoonfuls of olive oil, a teaspoonful of French made mustard, a level teaspoonful of salt and a saltspoonful of pepper. Boil four potatoes, cut them into blocks, and, when nearly cold, mix them with this dressing, and stand aside until very cold. Serve with a garnish of chopped celery or lettuce leaves.

This will serve six persons.

## MACEDOINE SALAD

A mixture of vegetables, peas, beans, carrots, turnips, can be purchased, canned, at any grocery store. Drain, wash them in cold water, dish them on a bed of shaved cabbage or lettuce leaves, and cover them with French dressing. All these vegetables may be cooked at home and used cold. String beans garnished with carrots make an excellent salad.

## BANANA SALAD

For this use the red bananas. Roll them out of the skin rather than strip the skin from them, and cut them into slices a half inch thick. Cover the bottom of your salad bowl with crisp lettuce leaves, then put over the bananas, allowing one banana to each two persons. Squeeze over the juice of a lemon, and, when ready to serve, baste with French dressing.

## APPLE AND NUT SALAD

4 tart apples
1 cupful of pecan meats
24 blanched almonds
2 sweet Spanish peppers
The rule for French dressing

Peel the apples, cut them into dice, squeeze over the juice of one or two lemons, and stand them aside until wanted. The lemon juice will prevent discoloration. Chop the nuts. At serving time line the salad bowl with a layer of chopped celery or cabbage or lettuce leaves, then a layer of apples, nuts, celery, apples and nuts. Baste with the French dressing, and, if you have them, garnish with the sweet peppers cut into strips, and use at once.

This, using a pint of chopped cabbage or celery, will serve six persons.

## CANTALOUPE SALAD

This is the newest and most sightly of salads. Arrange crisp lettuce or Romaine leaves on individual plates. Cut a cold ripe cantaloupe into halves, take out the seeds, and with a large vegetable scoop or teaspoon scoop out balls or egg-shaped pieces. Heap a half dozen of these on the lettuce leaves, and, at serving time, baste them well with French dressing, and serve. Watermelon may be substituted for cantaloupe.

# Sandwiches

Sandwiches may be made from thin white bread, or whole wheat bread, or Boston brown bread, or nut bread. A nut loaf is easily made at short notice, and needs only butter to make an excellent sandwich. An endless variety of sandwiches may be made from materials always at hand.

For CHEESE SANDWICHES: Grind or mash common American cheese, add a palatable seasoning of tomato catsup, Worcestershire sauce, and a little melted butter. A teaspoonful of these will be sufficient for a quarter of a pound of cheese. Put this between thin slices of unbuttered bread. If a large quantity of sandwiches is to be made, beat the butter to a cream before using it.

MEATS: All sorts of meats, just a little left over, may be chopped, seasoned and utilized for sandwiches. If the meat is slightly moistened with a little olive oil, cream or melted butter, and the sandwiches are wrapped in a damp cloth, as soon as made, and closed in a tin bread box, they will keep nicely for several hours.

On a warm day put a few moist lettuce leaves on top of the sandwiches, under the cloth, and put the box in a cold place.

Canned Salmon, Sardines, or boiled Salt Cod, pounded and nicely seasoned with oil and lemon juice, or mayonnaise, make nice sandwiches to serve with molded tomato jelly, and coffee, for a "winter evening." They are quite enough with coffee alone in an emergency.

Nut Sandwiches are made by putting chopped nuts or nut butter between thin slices of buttered bread, or crackers.

Sweet Sandwiches are made by putting a mixture of chopped fruits between thin slices of buttered bread. The fruits best suited for sandwiches are dates, raisins, candied ginger and cherries, and washed figs. These may be used separately or blended, using less ginger than other fruits. A nice filling may be made from a half pound of dates, an ounce of ginger, and ten cents' worth of roasted peanuts, or a quarter of a pound of pecans. Put these through a meat chopper, add the juice of an orange, and pack the mixture in jelly tumblers. Keep in a cold place. This will keep a month in winter, and equally long in a refrigerator in summer.

Sweet sandwiches are usually cut into "fingers," or into rounds with an ordinary biscuit cutter.

Honolulu Sandwiches are made by rubbing one roll of Neufchatel cheese with a half cupful of grated apple, two sweet Spanish peppers, and twenty-four blanched and chopped almonds. Add salt and a drop of Tabasco sauce. Spread between thin slices of unbuttered bread.

Jelly or Canned Fruit Sandwiches are made by spreading jelly or mashed fruit, drained, on a very thin slice of buttered bread. Trim off the crusts and roll quickly. Tie with baby ribbon, or press it firmly together. These are usually served with chocolate or tea.

Chicken Salad or Celery Mayonnaise Sandwiches are usually served with coffee, and can be made quickly by mixing any left-over chicken, or tender white celery, with mayonnaise, and putting the mixture between thin slices of buttered bread. A lettuce leaf on the bread first holds the salad nicely. One may use two lettuce leaves if necessary.

## NUT BREAD

- 2 cupfuls of flour
- ½ cupful of chopped nuts
- 2 teaspoonfuls of baking powder
- 1 cupful of milk
- 1 egg
- 2 tablespoonfuls of sugar
- ½ teaspoonful of salt

Sift the salt, baking powder and flour together, add and mix in the nuts and sugar. Beat the egg, add the milk, and stir these in the flour. Mix well, and turn it in a greased bread pan. Cover, and allow it to stand fifteen minutes. Bake in a moderately quick oven a half hour. Pecans, hickory nuts, peanuts, or English walnuts may be used.

Use the next day after it is baked. Cut thin, butter lightly, and press two slices together. Serve whole, or cut into halves. Do not remove the crusts.

# Suggestions for Church Suppers

## NUT MEAT ROLL

1 pound of chopped beef
1 quart of roasted peanuts in shells
1 teaspoonful of salt
1 saltspoonful of pepper
3 shredded wheat biscuits
2 eggs
1 tablespoonful onion juice
1 tablespoonful of parsley

Shell and chop the peanuts, mix them with the meat, and add the shredded wheat rubbed fine; salt, pepper, parsley, chopped, and onion juice. Mix well. Beat the egg slightly, add three tablespoonfuls of water, and mix this into the meat. Form in a roll about eight inches long, roll in oiled paper, place it in a baking pan, add a half cupful of water to the pan and bake in a moderate oven three quarters of an hour. Remove the paper and stand aside to cool. Serve in thin slices with either tomato or potato salad.

This will serve eight persons at a cost of about four cents each.

## JELLIED VEAL

3 knuckles of veal
4 onions
1 carrot
3 teaspoonfuls of salt
8 tablespoonfuls of vinegar
6 gherkins
1 teaspoonful of black pepper

Wash the knuckles, remove the meat and cut it in pieces. Put the bones in a kettle, the meat on top, and pour over six quarts of cold water. Bring to a boil, skim, and simmer gently two hours. Add the onion sliced, the carrot chopped, salt and pepper, and simmer one hour longer. Drain in a colander. Dip long molds, or ordinary bread pans, in cold water, cover the bottom with slices of hard boiled eggs, put the meat in bits on top of this, seasoning it with a little salt. Slice the gherkins and put them in layers between the meat. Strain the liquid, add the vinegar, and pour it over the meat. There should be just enough to cover it nicely. If there is more than this, boil it down before adding vinegar. Stand aside over night. When cold, dip the mold a second in boiling water, and turn the jelly in a platter. Serve cut in slices, with either a nice cold slaw, or cabbage and celery salad. Jellied beef is made the same, substituting a leg or shin of beef.

This will cost about seventy five cents, and will make twenty-five to thirty slices.

## BAGGED VEAL

2 pounds of lean ham
4 pounds of veal cutlet
3 shredded wheat biscuits
2 eggs
2 onions
1 teaspoonful of powdered sage
½ teaspoonful of allspice
1 teaspoonful of salt
½ teaspoonful of black pepper

Put the meat, raw, through a meat chopper, add the biscuits crumbed, the onions grated, and all the seasonings. Work it well with the hands, and mix in the eggs, slightly beaten. Pack the mixture in clean salt bags or bags about that size, plunge them in a kettle of boiling water, boil rapidly ten minutes, and simmer three hours. When cool, turn the bags wrong side out off the meat. Serve sliced like summer sausage.

This will cost one and a half dollars, and will serve twenty five persons.

## A SPANISH STEW FOR ONE HUNDRED PERSONS

25 pounds of round of beef
6 sweet peppers, or
1 can of Spanish pimentos
12 sweet turnips
½ bottle of Worcestershire sauce
1 cupful of flour
1 pound of suet
10 large onions
3 gallon cans of peas
12 carrots
1 jar of beef extract
4 tablespoonfuls of salt
4 tablespoonfuls of cornstarch
¼ pound of butter

Put the suet into a large kettle or in two smaller ones; try it out and remove the crackling. Add to the hot fat the onions and peppers chopped fine. Shake until they are well cooked and slightly browned. Add the meat cut into cubes of one inch, cover the kettles and cook a half hour, stirring now and then. Dissolve the beef extract in three gallons of hot water, pour it over the meat, and simmer for two hours. Add the carrots and turnips cut into dice, and more water if necessary, and cook one hour longer. Add the flour and cornstarch moistened in cold water, and all the seasonings. Stir and boil ten minutes, add the peas, drained, and serve. This is nice garnished with small hot milk biscuits. Taste before serving it, to see if you have added sufficient salt.

## VEAL ROLL

4 pounds of lean veal
3 shredded wheat biscuits
1 teaspoonful of salt
½ teaspoonful of sage
½ pound of lean ham
2 eggs
1 tablespoonful of parsley
1 saltspoonful of pepper

Put the veal and ham through a meat chopper, add all the seasonings, and the biscuits rubbed fine. Mix thoroughly, add the egg slightly beaten, mix again, and form into a roll three inches in diameter. Roll in oiled paper, place in a baking pan, cover the bottom of the pan with hot water, add a slice of onion, and, if you have it, a little chopped celery tops. Bake slowly one and a half hours, basting over the paper every fifteen minutes. When done, remove the paper, and put in a cold place. Serve in thin slices with tomato jelly salad.

This will cost about one dollar and will serve eighteen persons.

## MAN-OF-WAR SALAD

For twenty-five persons, chop sufficient hard white cabbage to make two quarts. Cover it with cold water, let it soak for an hour, and then wash it through several cold waters, and dry it in a towel. Cover three boxes of gelatin with a pint of cold water to soak a half hour. Open three cans of tomatoes, put them in a saucepan with four chopped onions, a cupful of chopped celery tops, if you have them, bring to a boil, add the juice of a lemon, a level tablespoonful of salt, ten drops of Tabasco sauce, the juice of a lemon, or two tablespoonfuls of vinegar, and the gelatin. Stir a moment, and press through a sieve. Dip bread pans or melon molds in cold water, put in a layer of cabbage, then a very thin layer of Indian relish, then cabbage, and so continue until the molds are filled. Pour over the tomato jelly, cold, and stand aside over night. Serve in slices with cooked or French dressing.

## COOKED DRESSING

Put a pint of milk over the fire in a double boiler, add three level tablespoonfuls of corn-starch moistened in a little cold milk. Cook until thick and smooth. Take from the fire, add the beaten yolks of four eggs, and work in slowly two tablespoonfuls of butter. Add a teaspoonful of salt and a saltspoonful of pepper. When cool add the juice of a lemon or four tablespoonfuls of vinegar. Fold in carefully the well-beaten whites of the eggs, and stand aside until very cold.

## GRANDMOTHER'S POTATO SALAD

Boil ten large potatoes in their jackets. Peel them and, when cool, cut eight into dice. Peel and mash the remaining two while hot; add to them a quarter pound of sweet butter, four tablespoonfuls of grated onion, two teaspoonfuls of salt, a dash of cayenne, two drops of Tabasco sauce, and press through a fine sieve. Hard boil two eggs; rub the yolks to a paste, and add two raw yolks. When smooth, add to these gradually the potato mixture. Thin to the consistency of good mayonnaise, with vinegar. At serving time mix the potato blocks and one can of drained peas with the dressing, being very careful not to break them. Dish on lettuce leaves, and garnish with chopped red beets, or, better, chopped celery. This is an excellent cheap salad, and will serve fifteen persons.

## SALMON PUDDING

Remove the bone, skin and oil from two pound cans of salmon. Boil together two cupfuls of white bread crumbs and one cupful of milk. Take from the fire, and add one cupful of boiled rice, a teaspoonful of salt, a saltspoonful of pepper, a teaspoonful of onion juice, and four eggs slightly beaten. Mix and work in the fish. Press the whole through a colander, and pack it at once into a mold. Cover and steam three-quarters of an hour. Serve hot with cream sauce.

This will serve twelve persons.

## NUT CAKE

At suppers where the yolks of eggs are used for mayonnaise or cooked dressing, the whites accumulate and are lost if not used in some white cake.

½ cupful of butter
2 cupfuls of flour
1½ cupfuls of sugar
¾ cupful of water
1 cupful of English walnut or hickory nut meats
2 rounding teaspoonfuls of baking powder
Whites of four eggs

Cream the butter, add the water and flour, alternately, beating all the while. Beat the whites, add half of them to the mixture, then all the nuts, chopped, then the baking powder, dry, and beat well. Fold in the remaining whites.

Bake in a round cake pan in a moderate oven three-quarters of an hour. When cool, ice the top and decorate it with nut meats.

## SCONES FOR TWENTY-FIVE PERSONS

Sift three quarts of flour with six rounding teaspoonfuls of baking powder and two of salt. Beat, without separating, three eggs. Rub into the flour a quarter of a pound of butter, or three tablespoonfuls of snowdrift. Add to the eggs one quart and a half of milk, and stir this into the flour. Mix quickly and drop by spoonfuls in greased baking pans, and bake fifteen minutes in a quick oven. Serve at once. These are better and more easily made than biscuits.

## POOR MAN'S FRUIT CAKE

3½ cupfuls of flour
1 cupful of brown sugar
½ cupful of New Orleans molasses
1 pound of seeded raisins
1 cupful of sour milk
½ cupful of butter
1 teaspoonful of cinnamon
1 teaspoonful of allspice
1 teaspoonful of soda

Cut the raisins into halves and flour them with four tablespoonfuls of the flour. Dissolve the soda in a tablespoonful of water, add it to the thick sour milk, beat a minute, add the molasses, beat again, add the butter, melted carefully, and stir in the flour; add the spices, and beat well. Stir in the raisins, and turn into a greased bread pan. Bake in a *moderate* oven one hour. When done, turn from the pan, baste with a syrup, made by boiling four tablespoonfuls of sugar with three of water, and add two teaspoonfuls of currant or grape jelly. Shut the cake in a tin box for a week or more. If made well this is moist and rich at very little cost.

## BANANA LAYER

¼ cupful of butter
1 cupful of sugar
2/3 cupful of water
2 cupfuls of flour
2 rounding teaspoonfuls of baking powder
Whites of four eggs

Put together the same as Ice Cream Cake, and bake in three layers. When cold, put together with Banana Filling.

## BANANA FILLING

Boil together one cupful of sugar and a half cupful of water until they spin a heavy thread, and pour slowly, beating all the while, into the well-beaten whites of two eggs. Beat until rather stiff and cold. When the cakes are cold, spread one-third of this filling over one cake, cover with thin slices of red bananas, put on another cake, on this another third of filling and bananas, and the remaining cake; cover this with the remaining filling, and dust thickly with chopped nuts. Do not let this stand too long, or the filling will absorb moisture from the bananas and run down the cake.

## ICE CREAM CAKE

1½ cupfuls of sugar
2½ cupfuls of flour
¼ cupful of butter
1 cupful of water
2 rounding teaspoonfuls of baking powder
Whites of five eggs

Cream the butter, adding slowly the sugar. Sift the flour with the baking powder. Add the water and flour alternately to the sugar mixture, and beat well. Fold in the well-beaten whites, and bake in three layers. Put together with a soft icing made from the whites of two eggs.

## FRUIT JELLY

Dip a fancy mold into cold water, fill it half full of mixed chopped candied fruits, or use dates, figs and bananas chopped. Fill the mold with a well-made lemon or orange gelatin. Serve plain, or with whipped cream.

## MOCK EGGS

½ box of gelatin
1 can pared apricots
1 cupful of sugar
1 pint of water
Whites of three eggs
Juice of three lemons

Cover the gelatin with a half cupful of cold water to soak for a half hour, add the sugar and the water boiling; stir until the gelatin is dissolved; add the lemon juice, strain, and cool until congealed but not too hard. Add the unbeaten whites of eggs, stand the bowl in a pan of cracked ice or cold water, and beat until the whole mass is as white as snow. Pour into ramekin dishes or paper cases, press a half apricot, rounding side up, in the centre, and stand aside in a cold place.

# Index

## ICE CREAMS, WATER ICES AND FROZEN PUDDINGS

# Index

## REFRESHMENTS FOR AFFAIRS